T0302066

Globalization and the Ethical Responsibilities of Multinational Corporations:

Emerging Research and Opportunities

Tarnue Johnson
Argosy University – Chicago, USA

A volume in the Advances in
Logistics, Operations, and
Management Science (ALOMS) Book
Series

www.igi-global.com

Published in the United States of America by
  IGI Global
  Business Science Reference (an imprint of IGI Global)
  701 E. Chocolate Avenue
  Hershey PA, USA 17033
  Tel: 717-533-8845
  Fax: 717-533-8661
  E-mail: cust@igi-global.com
  Web site: http://www.igi-global.com

Library of Congress Cataloging-in-Publication Data

Names: Johnson, Tarnue Carver, author.
Title: Globalization and the ethical responsibilities of multinational
  corporations : emerging research and opportunities / by Tarnue Johnson.
Description: Hershey, PA : Business Science Reference, [2017]
Identifiers: LCCN 2017004410| ISBN 9781522525349 (hardcover) | ISBN
  9781522525356 (ebook)
Subjects: LCSH: International business enterprises--Moral and ethical
  aspects--Africa. | Corporate governance--Africa. | Social responsibility
  of business--Africa. | Globalization.
Classification: LCC HD2917 .J64 2017 | DDC 174/.4--dc23 LC record available at https://lccn.loc.
gov/2017004410

This book is published in the IGI Global book series Advances in Logistics, Operations, and Management Science (ALOMS) (ISSN: 2327-350X; eISSN: 2327-3518)

British Cataloguing in Publication Data
A Cataloguing in Publication record for this book is available from the British Library.

All work contributed to this book is new, previously-unpublished material.
The views expressed in this book are those of the authors, but not necessarily of the publisher.

For electronic access to this publication, please contact: eresources@igi-global.com.

Advances in Logistics, Operations, and Management Science (ALOMS) Book Series

ISSN:2327-350X
EISSN:2327-3518

Editor-in-Chief: John Wang, Montclair State University, USA

MISSION

Operations research and management science continue to influence business processes, administration, and management information systems, particularly in covering the application methods for decision-making processes. New case studies and applications on management science, operations management, social sciences, and other behavioral sciences have been incorporated into business and organizations real-world objectives.

The **Advances in Logistics, Operations, and Management Science** (ALOMS) Book Series provides a collection of reference publications on the current trends, applications, theories, and practices in the management science field. Providing relevant and current research, this series and its individual publications would be useful for academics, researchers, scholars, and practitioners interested in improving decision making models and business functions.

COVERAGE

- Production management
- Information Management
- Organizational Behavior
- Computing and information technologies
- Risk Management
- Political Science
- Services management
- Networks
- Decision analysis and decision support
- Finance

IGI Global is currently accepting manuscripts for publication within this series. To submit a proposal for a volume in this series, please contact our Acquisition Editors at Acquisitions@igi-global.com or visit: http://www.igi-global.com/publish/.

Titles in this Series

For a list of additional titles in this series, please visit:
http://www.igi-global.com/book-series/advances-logistics-operations-management-science/37170

Optimal Management Strategies in Small and Medium Enterprises
Milan B. Vemić (Higher School of Academic Studies "DOSITEJ", Serbia)
Business Science Reference • ©2017 • 437pp • H/C (ISBN: 9781522519492) • US $225.00

Global Intermediation and Logistics Service Providers
Laurence Saglietto (Côte d'Azur University, France) and Cécile Cezanne (University Paris 13 Sorbonne Paris Cité, France)
Business Science Reference • ©2017 • 412pp • H/C (ISBN: 9781522521334) • US $210.00

Ethics and Sustainability in Global Supply Chain Management
Ulas Akkucuk (Bogazici University, Turkey)
Business Science Reference • ©2017 • 350pp • H/C (ISBN: 9781522520368) • US $200.00

Supply Chain Management in the Big Data Era
Hing Kai Chan (University of Nottingham Ningbo, China) Nachiappan Subramanian (University of Sussex, UK) and Muhammad Dan-Asabe Abdulrahman (University of Nottingham Ningbo, China)
Business Science Reference • ©2017 • 299pp • H/C (ISBN: 9781522509561) • US $195.00

Knowledge Management Initiatives and Strategies in Small and Medium Enterprises
Andrea Bencsik (Széchenyi István University, Hungary & J. Selye University, Slovakia)
Business Science Reference • ©2017 • 442pp • H/C (ISBN: 9781522516422) • US $200.00

Handbook of Research on Information Management for Effective Logistics...
George Leal Jamil (InescTec, Portugal) António Lucas Soares (University of Porto, Portugal) and Cláudio Roberto Magalhães Pessoa (FUMEC University, Brazil)
Business Science Reference • ©2017 • 554pp • H/C (ISBN: 9781522509738) • US $310.00

For an enitre list of titles in this series, please visit:
http://www.igi-global.com/book-series/advances-logistics-operations-management-science/37170

www.igi-global.com

701 East Chocolate Avenue, Hershey, PA 17033, USA
Tel: 717-533-8845 x100 • Fax: 717-533-8661
E-Mail: cust@igi-global.com • www.igi-global.com

Table of Contents

Preface

INTRODUCTION

The dawn of the 21st century has been profoundly influenced by tendencies of economic, political, cultural, institutional and technological forces under the impact of globalization. There is no doubt that modern Africa has not escaped the impact of these forces. The phenomenon of globalization has engendered conflicting outcomes in and between countries. Hence, while phenomenal economic growth has been recorded in some countries, those countries have also seen the gradual spread of economic and structural inequalities within their borders. Further, the gulf between Northern developed countries and poorer countries of the South, including Africa has widened due to globalization. In this context, one could view globalization as a zero-sum process (Stieglitz, 2002; Herath, 2008).

Thus, there is a consensus across the existing body of social science knowledge that globalizing processes have produced both positive and negative effects in the arenas of economic and social development in Africa and other developing regions of the world. The negative or positive outcomes of globalization have been emphasized selectively and to varying degrees depending on the ideological posture of the author (Giddens, 1990; Julius, 1997; Gills, 2000; Weber, 2002; Asiedu and Gyimah-Brempong, 2008). This is perhaps why Julius (1997, p. 453) posits that globalization is a portmanteau term, where the perspective and ideological posture of the author clearly matters.

The primary purpose of this book is to examine the nexus between globalization and the ethical responsibilities of multinational corporations (MNCs) in Africa. This researcher posits that through the prism of corporate governance broadly speaking, one is able to gauge the extent to which MNCs are meeting or neglecting their social and ethical responsibilities to their host countries. Because of this concern, the book focuses on the ethical underpinnings of the economic activities of multinational corporations (MNCs) in the context of globalization. Global cities are also focused upon in the postscript in an effort to explore the construct of global cities as one of the distinguishing characteristics of emerging patterns that have come to define present day globalization. In effect, globalization is being examined in this book in the context of how global and transnational firms have affected economic and social processes unfolding in Africa and other parts of the world.

ORGANIZATION OF THE BOOK

This book is divided into six chapters. Chapter one is the introductory chapter. Chapter two examines the turn from agency theory to stakeholder theory in the business ethics literature. Meanwhile, chapter three presents the result of some empirical investigations focusing on attempts to test the validity of stakeholder theory. This chapter also examines the activities of MNCs in Africa in the context of the analyses of foreign direct investment flows (FDI) to Africa.

The fourth chapter introduces critical theory by turning the discussion away from an enhanced stakeholder approach to critical stakeholder approaches. These approaches underscore the empowerment of stakeholders through communication processes on the basis of discourse ethics and moral reasoning. Chapter five summarizes the discussion in this book and presents some final thoughts. Thus, what these first five chapters underscore is that business ethics in a rapidly globalizing world is an essential part of the management curriculum.

Further, the chapters also emphasize the fact that managers with the responsibility for the foreign operations of MNCs are confronted with distinct ethical issues that may not necessarily arise in the operations of domestic firms. These may include issues such as the existence of diverse ethical traditions, economic organizations and legal and political systems. Levels of economic development, pervasive corruption and the fragility of institutional norms may also set developing countries in Africa apart from their counterparts in the developed world.

Chapter six is a postscript that provides an annotated bibliography on the themes of globalization and global city theory. This chapter presents an annotated bibliography of current trends regarding general perspectives and theoretical constructs on the spatial and temporal characteristics of globalization. Thus, this postscript also provides an annotated bibliography of current discussions and debates in the extant literature on the link between globalization and the historical evolution of global city theory. It is suggested that the discourse of global city and globalization has affected selected countries in Africa, both industrial and nonindustrial states as much as it has affected cities in other parts of the world.

As an annotated bibliography, the first section of this chapter presents academic resources that reflect general perspectives on globalization, including books, book chapters and peer reviewed journal articles. The rationale of providing information on global city theory consists in the fact that contemporary global cities are the major bases and urban cites that make the operations of MNCs in various parts of the world possible; they are also cites for the most globally transformative processes occurring that accentuate the accumulation of capital and that affect both the ethics and economics of MNCs.

In this light, the very phenomenon of globalization is impossible to make sense of adequately without given critical consideration to the dynamics of postmodern global cities in our 21st century world. This chapter also highlighted two empirical case studies of contemporary transformations that are shaping a current and an emerging global city. The aim of including these two cases is to highlight the diversity in ethical and strategic approaches to addressing the contingent challenges of global technological and structural transformations.

In this introductory chapter, this researcher has presented various definitions of globalization in the extant literature. Thus, the negative and positive effects of globalization are highlighted regarding the meaning and nature of this concept. This researcher shares the views of some authors (see, for example, Monshipouri, Welch and Kennedy, 2003) that the negative effects of globalization in Africa could be tempered through a combination of mandated corporate compliance with policies to strengthen African political and legal institutions.

This conclusion suggests that corporate compliance and ethical responsibilities should be mandated by activist states in Africa and not just left to voluntary self-regulation of MNCs operating on the continent. Corporate governance strategies, if they are to achieve any measure of success in tackling economic underdevelopment and inequality, must be facilitated and coordinated in partnerships with African governments (Gond, King & Moon, 2011). These assumptions build on insights from both the micro-foundations and political economy of globalization (Julius, 1997).

This book also considers theories of globalization and corporate governance by bringing competing theoretical accounts under critical scrutiny. One of the central tasks of this book is to speak to the need to provide some explanations regarding the path to stakeholder governance in Africa. Thus, it is suggested that stakeholder corporate governance is possible in Africa, like other parts of the world—only if implemented in partnerships with African governments and other relevant economic and political institutions—that would themselves be considered as stakeholders.

Readers will note that this book attempts to address two fundamentally interrelated research questions: 1) What does globalization mean for Africa in terms of the ethical dimensions of the operations of MNCs? 2) How to create a new path to stakeholder governance in Africa to make globalization a win-win proposition for all stakeholders involved in the activities of MNCs? This researcher sought to address these questions in subsequent chapters of this book.

METHODS AND SOURCES

The accounts presented in this chapter relied on both primary and secondary sources. Secondary sources included books and peer reviewed journal articles that define the literature on globalization broadly and also on the issue of the ethical responsibilities of business in the context of globalization. Primary sources included various statistical reports regarding international trade flows found on the website of the United Nations Trade and Development Organization. Findings reflected in both primary and secondary data sources presented in this discussion provide justification and rationale for my analyses regarding the current state of knowledge and theoretical developments on the topic of the ethical dimensions of the operations of MNCs in Africa; a topic which falls under the rubric of business ethics. Social science methods applied to public policy questions have also been applied in this book.

GLOBALIZATION DEFINED

Globalization in the modern world is an all-encompassing term. The term globalization also correlates with social and political change occurring in the context of technological change (Weber, 2002). Globalization is all encompassing because it embraces the system of economic, political, cultural and social relations that characterize the present world system. Thus, globalization describes the multiplicity of linkages and interdependencies that exist between states and societies that make up the present world system (Dunning, 1997). These views are shared by other authors (Alice, 2001; Guvenli and Sanyal, 2002; Kieh, 2016).

For example, Alice (2001, p. 16) refers to globalization as being a multifaceted and multidimensional phenomenon that "intermingles economics, politics, and culture." Hence, globalization is viewed as a higher degree of internationalization (p. 16). Anthony Giddens (1990, p. 63) suggests that the very process of modernity itself is inherently globalizing. Globalization has unleashed a process where trade, investment and capital flows intensify ties between nations (Alice, 2000, p. 16).

Landau (2001, p. 34) indicates that for Bairoch and Kozul-Wright (1997) the ingredients of globalization includes "open markets, transnational corporations, and new information technologies." For the purpose of this book, and following in the lead of Dunning (1997, pp. 13-14) one could distinguish two forms of economic globalization: the shallowest form of globalization and the deepest form. The shallowest form leads to a situation where a typical global firm engages in arms-length trade in a single product within another economic entity in one other country.

Then there is the deepest form of globalization. This form involves a process where an economic entity transacts with a large number of other economic entities across a network of value-chains to serve its worldwide interests (p. 15). The deepest form of globalization appropriately describes the nature of the activities of MNCs on the African continent (p. 15). The pressures of competition--from competitors and consumers alike--make companies to search for new markets and raw materials (p. 15). Other economic forces such as the escalating costs of research and development (R&D) and increasingly truncated product life circles have compelled companies to search for wider markets (p. 15).

In short, the global expansion of MNCs in Africa suggests that they do not operate in the perfectly competitive equilibrium of microeconomic theory but rather in the turbulent world of Schumpeter's 'creative destruction' (Julius, 1997). National governments and regional authorities in Africa and other developing regions of the world have aided globalization through the pursuance of economic liberalization under neo-liberal policy regimes. Critics claim that increased interaction and the globalization of world markets--embraced by MNCs and home country governments--have created unfavorable economic conditions in African countries. Monshipouri, Welch and Kennedy (2003) concurred with these criticisms

The MNCs' power to control international investment, especially portfolio investments, has had enormous bearing on the economies of developing countries. Faced with pressures to attract such investments, governments in the South have had little or no alternative but to be receptive to the terms of MNCs. The lack of leverage with the MNCs has meant, for example, that minimum wage has been set unrealistically low in developing countries so as to attract foreign investment. A related criticism of MNCs is that their overall strategy to relocate from the North has kept wages and living conditions down and resulted in the expansion of sweatshops in the South (p. 966).

Conceptions of globalization are supported by classical development theory and conventional neoclassical trade theory. These conceptions are grounded in the theory of comparative advantage, which argues that global economic expansion does not necessarily produce zero-sum outcomes (Herath, 2008). Implicit in this theory is the assumption that both developed and underdeveloped economies will be better off as they choose to produce the cheapest possible goods and services (p. 821). Julius (1997, p. 453) argues that conventional economic theory sees globalization as an "end-state of a fully integrated world market."

Julius also asserts that political scientists define globalization as a process where non-state actors, like MNCs, assume an increasing proportion of power and influence in the shaping of world order (p. 453). Haslam (2007) generally agrees with this assertion. Lunga (2008, p.191) also reaffirms this thesis when she asserts that "to be useful the relationship between postcolonial and globalization theory must be "conceptualized in actual historical and political contexts not disconnected from actual issues of power."

This notion that globalization has increased the power of non-state actors in the face of the state's retreat from a previous interventionist role is reinforced by critics who argued that the removal of trade barriers encouraged MNCs to locate to African countries to take advantage of lower labor costs and the absence of enforceable regulations (Guvenli and Sanyal, 2002). When referring to what he calls 'some of the real downsides' of foreign investment, Joseph Stiglitz (2002) argues that

When foreign businesses come in they often destroy local competitors, quashing the ambitions of the small businessmen who had hoped to develop into manufacturers around the world (p. 68).

Other conceptions of globalization see the subordination of states, values and institutions as part of the strategic aim of globalization (Gills, 2000; Weber, 2002). Gills (2000) locates the meaning of globalization in the context of a politics of resistance and a critique of neo-liberal ideology. Thus, Gills (p. 4) puts forward four defining characteristics, when globalization is contextualized in terms of neo-liberal economic globalization:

- Protection of the interests of capital and expansion of the process of capital accumulation on world scale;
- A tendency towards homogenization of state policies and state forms to render them instrumental to the protection of capital and the process of capital accumulation on world scale, via a new 'market ideology';
- The formation and expansion of a new tier of transnationalized institutional authority above the state's, which has the aim and purpose of re-articulating states to the purpose of facilitating global capital accumulation; and
- The political exclusion of dissident social forces from the arena of state policy-making, in order to desocialize the subject and insulate the neoliberal state from against the societies over which they preside, thus facilitating the socialization of risk on behalf of capital.

Chanda (2008) focuses on the issue of governance and stresses that governance infrastructures have lagged behind the pace of globalization thus resulting in problems and conflicts. Chanda posits that globalization has been with us since the dawn of history but the idea of trying to govern the interconnections that it has produced through trade, travel, and interaction, have lagged far behind. Globalization (Mittelman, 2002) is also perceived as posing a challenge to the Westphalian model of states that was established in the West and grafted on to other parts of the world:

Globalization calls into question the ability of the existing interstate system to cope with certain fundamental transactional problems. After all, the Westphalian model of states is a relic of the seventeenth century, established in the West and grafted on to other parts of the world. Strains on this system include the properties of technologies- interconnectivity and lightning speed- as well as massive concentrations of private economic power that dwarf the resources of many national units and challenge state sovereignty (p. 9).

Gucenli and Sanyal (2002) argue that as the world economy has become integrated, so has the grievance and backlash against globalization. The authors further argue, drawing their clues from critics of the process of global integration that this process has led to the loss of high-paying jobs in developed countries and increased exploitation of workers in developing countries. The November 1999 protest---in the United States City of Seattle, Washington—when demonstrators scuttle planned negotiations by the World Trade Organization (WTO) to expand global trade—is cited as a prime example of outrage against globalization, particularly in the developed world (p. 195-196).

Indeed, widespread dissatisfaction against some of the economic and social consequences of globalization are being currently felt in the ongoing presidential elections in the United States. Strine (2008) reinforces these sentiments in his reference to the level of discomfort and unease with globalization in the United States

Discomfort with globalization is widespread in the United States. Discomfort, I think, is the right word. We're not shutting the borders any time soon, but unease is widespread across the political spectrum. There is a sense that we are losing control of our own dismay and the ability to provide economic security and stability to our citizens, but we seem to lack the political vocabulary and maturity to discuss what is facing us in any but the crudest of terms. Thus, cartoonish debates between straw-man concepts- like free trade versus protectionism, and closed versus open borders- abound, with simplistic nostrums substituted for hard thought (p. 256).

REFERENCES

Adams, S., & Mengistu, B. (2008). The political economy of privatization in sub-Saharan Africa. *Social Science Quarterly, 89*(1), 78–94. doi:10.1111/j.1540-6237.2008.00522.x

Alice, L. (2001). *Redrawing the global economy: Elements of integration and fragmentation.* New York: Palgrave.

Asiedu, E., & Gyimah-Brempong, K. (2008). *The effect of the liberalization of investment policies on employment and investment of multinational corporations in Africa. African Development Bank.* Oxford: Blackwell Publishing Ltd.

Bairoch, P., & Kozul-Wright, R. (1996). *Globalization myths: Some historical reflections on integration, industrialization and growth in world economy.* UNCTAD, Geneva.

Boafo-Arthur, K. (2003). Tackling Africa's developmental dilemmas: Is globalization the Answer? *Journal of Third World Studies, 20*(1), 27–54.

Dunning, J. H. (1997). The advent of alliance capitalism. In J. H. Dunning & K. A. Hamdani (Eds.), *The new globalism and developing countries* (pp. 12–50). Tokyo: United Nations Press.

Giddens, A. (1990). *The consequences of modernity.* Cambridge: Polity Press.

Gills, B. K. (2000). Introduction: Globalization and the politics of resistance. In B. K. Gills (Ed.), *Globalization and the politics of resistance.* Houndmills: Macmillan Press LTD. doi:10.1057/9780230519176_1

Guvenli, T., & Sanyal, R. (2002). Ethical concerns in international business: Are some issues more important than others? *Business and Society Review, 107*(2), 195–206. doi:10.1111/1467-8594.00132

Haslam, P. A. (2007). The firm rules: Multinational corporations, policy space and neoliberalism. *Third World Quarterly, 28*(6), 1167–1183. doi:10.1080/01436590701507594

Herath, D. (2008). Development discourse of the globalists and dependency theorists: Do the globalization theorists rephrase and reword the central concepts of the dependency school? *Third World Quarterly, 29*(4), 819–834. doi:10.1080/01436590802052961

Julius, D. (1997). Globalization and stakeholder conflicts: A corporate perspective. *International Affairs, 73*(3), 453–468. doi:10.2307/2624267

Kieh, G. K. (2016). Africa and economic globalization. In E. L. Wonkeryor (Ed.), *Globalization and its implications for Africa.* New Jersey: Africana Homestead Legacy Publishers.

Landau, A. (2001). *Rewarding the global economy: Elements of integration and fragmentation.* Hampshire: Palgrave. doi:10.1057/9780230511361

Lunga, V. B. (2008). Postcolonial theory: A language for a critique of globalization? *Perspectives on Global Development and Technology, 7*(3/4), 191–199. doi:10.1163/156914908X371349

Mittelman, J. H. (2002). Making globalization work for the have nots. *International Journal on World Peace, 19*(2), 3–25.

Monshipouri, M., Welch, C. E., & Kennedy, E. T. (2003). Multinational corporations and the ethics of global responsibility: Problems and possibilities. *Human Rights Quarterly, 25*(4), 965–989. doi:10.1353/hrq.2003.0048

Stiglitz, J. E. (2002). *Globalization and its discontents*. New York: W.W. Norton Company.

Strine, L. E. Jr. (2008). Human freedom and two Friedmen: Musings on the implications of Globalization for the effective regulation of corporate behavior. *University of Toronto Law Journal, 58*(3), 241–274. doi:10.3138/utlj.58.3.241

Weber, R. (2002). Extracting value from the city: Neolibralism and urban redevelopment. *Antipode: A radical. The Journal of Geography, 34*(3), 519–540.

ADDITIONAL READING

Diehl, P. F., & Frederking, B. (2010). *The politics of global governance: International organizations in an interdependent world*. Boulder: Lynne Rienner Publishers.

Dunning, J. (2003). *Making globalization good: The moral challenges of global capitalism*. Oxford: Oxford University Press. doi:10.1093/0199257019.001.0001

Hass, P. M., & Hird, J. A. (Eds.). (2013). *Controversies in globalization: Contending approaches to international relations*. Los Angeles: Sage Publications. doi:10.4135/9781506335407

Taylor, S. D. (2012). *Globalization and the cultures of business in Africa: From patrimonialism to profit*. Bloomington: Indiana University Press.

Weinstein, M. M. (2005). *Globalization: what's new?* New York: Columbia University Press.

Chapter 1
Introduction

INTRODUCTION

This book could not have come at an opportune time when the issues of the economic, social, cultural and technological consequences of globalization could be said to have now occupied a crucial space in the corridors of international trade relations and contemporary intellectual and social theory. One would note that as expected this space has been occupied both by critics and supporters of globalization, each side marshalling their claims to justify their preferred policy options, predispositions and perceived normative courses of action.

However, in this debate the specific question of how globalization has affected the menu of choices and strategic options facing multinational corporations (MNCs) operating on the African continent has received little attention. One would argue that host governments in Africa also need relevant information to inform their development strategies and attitudes about how to approach MNCs. This book is an attempt to provide some answers to this essential question. The first three chapters of the book highlight various issues ranging from a working definition of globalization and how the construct itself can be used to explain contemporary economic affairs in Africa as they relate to the issue of marginalization of much of the continent's peoples.

The chapters also highlight a discussion of the critical turn in modern management discourse from agency theory to stakeholder theory. Further, the chapters include a presentation of various attempts to test the validity of stakeholder theory. Finally, activities of MNCs in Africa are examined in the context of the analyses of foreign direct investment flows (FDI) to Africa

DOI: 10.4018/978-1-5225-2534-9.ch001

within a specified period. The last three chapters are both descriptive and prescriptive. Thus, the issue of what African countries should do in fulfilling their tasks of designing appropriate public policies to provide a pathway to economic development somewhat unencumbered by the trappings of the current global economic order is addressed in the remaining two chapters of the book. These chapters introduced a discussion of critical theory by turning the discussion away from an enhanced stakeholder approach to critical stakeholder approaches. It was suggested that these approaches underscore the empowerment of stakeholders through communication processes on the basis of discourse ethics and moral reasoning.

Thus, what the chapters underscore is that business ethics in a rapidly globalizing world should become an essential part of the management curriculum. The book also emphasizes the fact that managers and other corporate leaders----with the responsibility for the foreign operations of MNCs----are confronted with distinct ethical issues that may not necessarily arise in the operations of domestic firms. These may include issues such as the existence of diverse ethical traditions, economic organizations and legal and political systems.

This researcher notes that levels of economic development, pervasive corruption and the fragility of institutional norms may also set developing countries in Africa apart from their counterparts in the developed world. The postscript should be viewed as constituting part of the overarching conceptual framework of the book as it provides an annotated bibliography of current discussions and debates in the extant literature on the link between globalization and the historical evolution of global city theory. It is suggested that the empirical link between global cities and globalization has manifestly affected selected countries in Africa, both industrial and nonindustrial states as much as it has affected cities in other parts of the world. This suggestion also presupposes that global city theory says as much about the role of global cities in understanding the activities of MNCs as it is about their ethical and moral predispositions.

Another critical issue that resonated throughout this book is the contention that the voices of all stakeholders should be heard in regulating interpersonal affairs and conflicts in the context of the operations of firms and other organizational forms. The book also upholds the notion that the basic question as to which way to proceed in determining the proper fit between the profit motive of firms and the long-term welfare of ordinary citizens must be decided upon through discursive processes of legitimation. This researcher hopes that this book will become a vital tool for those interested in exploring the essential nexus between globalization, corporate governance and the role global cities play in capitalist accumulation as the cites, where MNCs are located. The researcher also hopes that by reading this book and critically distilling its content---business and management scholars will be able to come to terms with some of the complex issues involved in making sense of and disentangling relevant empirical facts---as they relate to the consequences of globalization and the complexity of economic and structural change--- unfolding in contemporary African countries.

This book concludes that globalization has increased the gulf between rich and poor countries in terms of levels of income growth and socio-economic development. Economic and structural inequalities within countries have also increased as a result of globalization. In cognizance of these consequences, the author notes that globalization requires some modification both at the level of business practice and at the level of its various theoretical conceptualizations. It is suggested that at the level of the firm some of the negative effects of globalization could be addressed through both an enhanced and critical stakeholder approach to corporate governance. The book encapsulates the perspective that ethical challenges facing MNCs are difficult to truly understand without an understanding of some of the moral imperatives that cities and policy makers face. The book concludes that organizational collaboration through objective rational discourse can amplify a positive feedback loop consistent with the desire to ensure technical efficiency and adherence to ethical norms and standards of right conduct.

Chapter 2
From Agency Theory to Stakeholder Theory

INTRODUCTION

This chapter concerns itself with elaborating on the epistemic distinctions between agency theory and contemporary stakeholder theory. The chapter first draws readers' attention to the inequality and lack of fairness in an evolving global system under the aegis of economic globalization. One of the main conclusions of this chapter is that globalization requires some modification both at the level of business practice and at the level of its various theoretical conceptualizations. The chapter draws on the discussion of various authors who have emphasized the notion that perhaps a critical stakeholder approach to the theory of the firm might help modify existing theoretical perspectives. It is suggested that these alternative theoretical explanations and paradigms might also help to correct our understanding of some of the deleterious effects of the operations of MNCs in Africa and elsewhere in the developing world.

AGENCY THEORY AND STAKEHOLDER THEORY

Protests against globalization are not entirely about the mere fact of globalization. The key issue at stake is the level of inequality and lack of fairness in a world system that globalization has given rise to. This indicates that the distribution of benefits or economic gains from globalization linked to the activities of MNCs requires modification (Sen, 2002). One would submit

DOI: 10.4018/978-1-5225-2534-9.ch002

that countries in Africa and other parts of the developing world have suffered dearly from this lack of fairness under the regime of globalization. Thus, these historical and structural iniquities crystallize the need for consolidating corporate governance frameworks to reflect the aspirations of all relevant stakeholders in Africa and in other parts of the world, where most of those excluded from the current economic gains of globalization live.

Thus, one would suggest that theories of corporate governance linked to the micro-level foundations of firms provide valuable insights into some of the issues at stake. In an article by Garriga and Mele (2004, p. 51) the authors conclude that the *Corporate Social Responsibility* (CSR) field presents a landscape of theories and approaches. Thus, the authors categorized CSR theories and main approaches in four groups:

- Instrumental theory, in which the corporation is seen as only an instrument for wealth creation, and its social activities are only a means to achieve economic results;
- Political theories, which concern themselves with the power of corporations in society and a responsible use of this power in the political arena;
- Integrative theories, in which the corporation is focused on the satisfaction of social demands; and
- Ethical theories, based on ethical responsibilities of corporations to society.

INSTRUMENTAL, INTEGRATIVE, AND ETHICAL THEORIES

Among other tasks, the researcher shall provide some accounts of two contrasting ethical theories of the firm that fall under the classification above: agency theory and stakeholder theory. Both theories, while working within the same ideological framework of managerial capitalism, have nevertheless, arrived at contrasting conclusions regarding the nature of the modern corporation (Freeman, 2005).

The ideological foundations of agency theory have been faulted for their lack of consideration of the diversity in corporate governance regimes (Triantis and Daniels, 1995). Agency theory has proclaimed shareholder interests to be the 'general interest' because they are assumed to be the most appropriate interests suited to make decisions about corporate strategy (Horn, 2012, p. 86). The interests of other groups, such as labor interests, do not feature in the prescription of agency theory for the formation of efficient governance structures "as the relationship between management and labor is assumed to be settled contractually." (p. 86). Horn (p. 85) observed "Following Coase's work on the theory of the firm, agency theory was preoccupied with ways to resolve the principal-agent conflicts resulting from the separation of ownership from control."

It is suggested that because labor and other groups have no interests in corporate control, there is no need including them in regulation and corporate governance arrangements. Thus, agency theory prescribes that state or public intervention should only be tolerated where it serves to address market failures. These views are usually supported by advocates of laissez-faire capitalism and the postulates of agency theory. The most prominent exponent was the late Milton Friedman of the University of Chicago.

In 1962 Friedman put forward a shareholder primacy perspective, solely focusing on the firm's responsibility to its owners (Munilla & Miles, 2005). In *Capitalism and Freedom*, Friedman (cited in Munilla & Miles, 2005, p. 372) asserted that "Few trends would so thoroughly undermine the very foundations of our free society as the acceptance by corporate officials of a social responsibility other than to make as much money for their stockholders as they possibly can." Friedman (Nehme & Wee, 2008, p. 132) opposed the idea that businesses had corporate social responsibility for the following reasons:

- Corporations, unlike real people, cannot be said to have social responsibilities;
- Company directors are merely shareholders' agents; hence their sole purpose should be to maximize shareholders' wealth;
- Company directors, not being the owners of corporations, do not have the right to spend shareholders' money on matters that are not related to profit-generating; and
- It is difficult to decide the appropriate social duties corporations should be responsible for, since one man's good is another's evil.

Freidman was adamantly opposed to a stakeholder primacy perspective. He could not see an expanded vision of management beyond the profit maximization function (Orts and Strudler, 2002; 2009). In line with the premises of agency theory, Freidman was of the view that managers lack competence and legitimacy to pursue ends that were at odds with corporate profits (Strine, 2008). Such an action, he believed, would undermine the "obvious utility of the corporate form and pervert the democratic process by having managers use other people's money for social purposes of their own choosing." (p. 257). These statements presupposed that the notion of social responsibilities that arise from economic inequality associated with the activities of firms belongs to a different domain- the redistributive functions of government- rather than agents acting on behalf of stockholders.

Far better, Friedman believed, for these managers- who were hardly representative of the general populace- to stick to their knitting. If they ran profitable operations, the wealth that was created could be, if government chose, redistributed to temper economic inequality. But it was not the job of corporate managers to be agents for their idiosyncratic visions of the overall social good. Rather, they were to vigorously pursue profits for stockholders, tempered only by the requirement to comply with laws and generally accepted business norms (p. 257).

However, an alternative stakeholder theory counter's these assumptions. A stakeholder primacy perspective has expanded the notion of a firm's obligations to all relevant stakeholders (Munilla & Miles, 2005). Unlike the stockholder primacy perspective, this perspective holds that top management plays a crucial role in safeguarding the welfare of the corporation through balancing the multiple claims of conflicting stakeholders (Freeman, 2002, p. 218).

Freeman (2002, p. 218) insists that "the normative, descriptive, instrumental and metaphorical uses of stakeholder theory are tied together in particular political constructions to yield a number of possible stakeholder theories." Freeman puts forward a teleological perspective with regards to the central purpose of the firm in stakeholder theory.

A stakeholder theory of the firm must redefine the purpose of the firm. The stockholder theory claims that the purpose of the firm is to maximize the welfare of the stockholders, perhaps subject to some moral or social constraints, either because such maximization leads to the greatest good or because of property rights. The purpose of the firm is quite different in my view (p. 218).

Thus, stakeholder theory is an extension of the view that doing business is more than making money (Orts & Strudler, 2002). The theory has its antecedents in ideas of corporate social responsibility. Like earlier ideas of corporate social responsibility, stakeholder theory is intended to expand the vision of management "of its roles and responsibilities beyond the profit maximization function to include interests and claims of non-stockholding groups." (p. 216).

Orts and Strudler (p. 216) suggest that Edward Freeman has developed the most received version of who counts as a stakeholder: "A stakeholder in an organization is (by definition) any group or individual who can affect or is affected by the achievement of the organization's objectives." This is the "broad definition" of who is a stakeholder. There is the "narrow definition", which Freeman (2005, p. 115) claims include groups that are vital to the survival and success of the corporation. Orts and Strudler (2002) conclude that the broad definition of who is a stakeholder is so expansive that it could be rendered meaningless.

This definition is also regarded as so complex that it could be rendered useless. This lack of precise definition of who is a stakeholder in the broader sense in an organization stems from the fact that the economic interests recognized in stakeholder theory often conflict, while the theory itself offers no convincing way to reconcile these conflicting interests. It is suggested that Freeman himself recognized this problem in an article coauthored with William Evan:

Management, especially top management, must look after the health of the corporation, and this involves balancing the multiple claims of conflicting stakeholders. Owners want more financial returns, while customers want more money spent on research and development. Employees want higher wages and better benefits, while local community wants better parks and day-care facilities (p. 218).

On the basis of the foregoing observation, Orts and Strudler (2002) conclude that stakeholder theory provides an explanation of those who have an economic stakes at risk in a corporation to include non-equity owners such as employees, various types of creditors and others. The authors call for limiting the concept of a stakeholder to include only those who have "actual economic stakes" in a firm (p. 227). It is suggested that this approach would allow for recognizing and giving careful consideration to important and salient ethical issues to be addressed directly and practically, without the unnecessary baggage of an unworkable theory, such as the effects of business practices and decisions on the natural environment and communities as well (p. 227).

In fact, Orts and Strudler (2002) also claim that the issues of environmental protection are examples of important ethical questions that cannot be reduced to a balancing exercise of competing interests of business participants. In an article by Donaldson and Preston (1995) the authors identified three different schools of stakeholder theory: (1) descriptive, (2) instrumental, and (3) normative. Preuss (2008) also conducts an elaborate analysis of these various strands of stakeholder theory.

This researcher agrees with Donaldson and Preston's conclusion as reechoed in Orts and Strudler (2002) that stakeholder theory requires a normative philosophical foundation because merely following the interest of stakeholders does not always lead to ethical results. In fact, an enhanced stakeholder approach that balances off the interests of stakeholders in MNCs through the instrumentalities of an enlightened African state is inherently a normative perspective. Jones (1995) has addressed the need for put forward an integrative approach. The author argues that stakeholder theory can be enhanced as an overarching theme that ingrates the business and society field. Such an approach, the author claims, would be based on a synthesis of the stakeholder concept, economic theory, behavioral science, and ethics.

In another article by Jones (1996) the author proposes a novel way of theorizing about business organizations that leads to the development of instrumentally and normatively convergent stakeholder theory. The author suggests that this form of theory will end of being explicitly normative, demonstrating how managers can create morally sound approaches to business and make them work.

Donaldson and Preston (1995) suggest that stakeholder theory has been put forward and justified in the management literature on the basis of its descriptive accuracy, instrumental power, and normative validity. It is suggested that these three types of argument has different implications. Hence, the three aspects of stakeholder theory are said to be mutually supportive and that the normative foundation of the theory, which is said to include property rights are fundamental.

Key (1999) claims that current conceptualizations of stakeholder theory may yet equal to an appropriate model that describes firm behavior. However, it is also suggested that they do not meet the requirements of a scientific theory. The author suggests that contractual interest may underlie stakeholder relationships just as they do agency-relationships between managers and stockholders as prescribed by traditional economic theory. Trevino and Weaver (1999) dwell on questions concerning the validity of a convergent stakeholder theory that would allow the theoretical integration of stakeholder research.

The authors claim that the proposed convergent theory lacks empirically testable constructs and explanatory relationships associated with established scientific theories. The authors intimate that a stakeholder research tradition should be one that incorporates shared concepts and normative concerns for organizational stakeholder relations. Jawahar and Mclaughlin (2001) integrate theory and research from many areas to develop a descriptive stakeholder theory.

This theoretical approach is perceived as one that examines stakeholder relationships on the basis of an organizational life cycle approach. Thus, the authors propose that at any given organizational life cycle stage, certain stakeholders will be more important than others. Hence, the authors identify specific stakeholders that they claim would become more salient as the organization evolves from one state to the next.

It is suggested that the strategy that an organization uses to deal with each stakeholder will be dependent upon the importance of that stakeholder to the organization relative to other stakeholders. Thomas Donaldson (1999) puts forward a method of unifying stakeholder theory. The author argues that two methodological approaches to stakeholder theory, instrumental and normative, converge, with instrumental versions hinging upon hypothetical claims in terms of the best route to achieve set objectives and goals, while normative versions hinging upon ethical claims. One of the claims of Donaldson (1999) is that there is logic that can line normative and empirical beliefs together. It is suggested that this link that brings together normative and instrumental domains of stakeholder theory lies inside the minds of corporate executives.

An article by Mitchell, Agle and Wood (1997) aims to contribute to a theory of stakeholder identification and salience based on stakeholders possessing one or more of three relationship attributes: power, legitimacy, and urgency. The authors suggest that by integrating the three, a typology of stakeholders could be generated. On the basis of this typology, the authors also put forward series of propositions to be considered by managers of firms. Jones, Felps and Gregory (2007) claim to use convergent elements of major ethical theories to create a typology of beliefs, values and practices that have evolved for solving problems and managing stakeholder relationship.

The authors described five stakeholder cultures—corporate egoist, agency, instrumentalist, moralist, and altruist. It is suggested that these organizational cultures lie on a continuum, ranging from individually self-interested (agency culture) to fully other regarding (altruist culture). It is also suggested that this approach could help refine stakeholder salience theory. Philips (2003) for his part has drawn a distinction between normative and derivative legitimacy. The author suggests that reference to this distinction helps to differentiate between a relationship within the organization based on direct moral obligation and one informed by the power to assist or harm the organization.

CONCLUSION

This chapter concerned itself with elaborating on the crucial distinctions between agency theory and contemporary stakeholder theory. Thus, one of the main conclusions of this chapter is that globalization requires some modification both at the level of business practice and at the level of its various theoretical conceptualizations. The chapter dwelt into the various features of an integrated or convergent stakeholder theory that addresses the crucial concerns of the various classes of agents who have a stake in the operations of MNCS. One would observe that these concerns are given voice to in the business ethics literature, especially when one examines the discussion of various authors, who have emphasized the notion that perhaps a critical stakeholder approach to the theory of the firm might enhance the overarching normative, strategic, and instrumental considerations that underlie the stakeholder theoretical model and other approaches that extol the ethical responsibilities of firms.

REFERENCES

Donaldson, T. (1999). Making stakeholder theory whole. *Academy of Management Review*, 24(2), 237–241. doi:10.2307/259079

Donaldson, T., & Preston, L. E. (1995). The stakeholder theory of the corporation: Concepts, evidence, and implications. *Academy of Management Review*, 20, 65–91.

Garriga, E., & Melé, D. (2004). Corporate social responsibility theories: Mapping the territory. *Journal of Business Ethics*, 53(1-2), 51–71. doi:10.1023/B:BUSI.0000039399.90587.34

Horn, L. (2012). *Regulating corporate governance in the EU*. London: Palgrave Macmillan. doi:10.1057/9780230356405

Jawahar, M., & Mclaughlin, G. C. (2001). Toward a descriptive theory: An organizational life cycle approach. *Academy of Management Review, 26*(3), 397–414.

Jones, T. M. (1995). Instrumental stakeholder theory: A synthesis of ethics and economics. *Academy of Management Review, 20*(2), 404–437.

Jones, T. M., Felps, W., & Bigley, G. A. (2007). Ethical theory and stakeholder related decisions: The role of stakeholder culture. *Academy of Management Review, 32*(1), 137–155. doi:10.5465/AMR.2007.23463924

Jones, T. M., & Wicks, A. C. (1996). Convergent stakeholder theory. *Academy of Management Review, 24*(2), 206–224.

Key, S. (1999). Toward a new theory of the firm: A critique of stakeholder theory. *Management Decision, 37*(4), 317–328. doi:10.1108/00251749910269366

Mitchell, R., Agle, B. K., & Wood, D. J. (1997). Toward a theory of stakeholder identification and salience: Defining the principle of who and what really counts. *Academy of Management Review, 22*(4), 853–886.

Munilla, L. S., & Miles, M. P. (2005). The corporate social responsibility continuum as a component of stakeholder theory. *Business and Society Review, 110*(4), 371–387. doi:10.1111/j.0045-3609.2005.00021.x

Nehme, M., & Wee, C. K. G. (2008). Tracing the historical development of corporate social responsibility and corporate social reporting. *James Cook University Law Review, 15*, 129–168.

Orts, E. W., & Strudler, A. (2002). The ethical and environmental limits of stakeholder theory. *Business Ethics Quarterly, 12*(2), 215–233. doi:10.2307/3857811

Orts, E. W., & Strudler, A. (2009). Putting a stake in stakeholder theory. *Business Ethics Quarterly, 88*(S4), 605–615. doi:10.1007/s10551-009-0310-y

Philips, R. (2003). Stakeholder legitimacy. *Business Ethics Quarterly, 13*(1), 25–41. doi:10.5840/beq20031312

Preuss, L. (2008). A reluctant stakeholder? On the perception of corporate social responsibility among European unions. *Business Ethics (Oxford, England), 17*(2), 149–160. doi:10.1111/j.1467-8608.2008.00528.x

Sen, A. (2001, July 15). It's fair, it's good, thoughts about globalization. *International Herald Tribune.*

Strine, L.E. Jr. (2008). Human freedom and two Friedmen: Musings on the implications of Globalization for the effective regulation of corporate behavior. *University of Toronto Law Journal, 58*(3), 241–274. doi:10.3138/utlj.58.3.241

Trevino, L. K., & Weaver, G. R. (1999). The stakeholder research tradition: Converging theorists—not converging theory. *Academy of Management Review, 24*(2), 222–227. doi:10.2307/259076

Triantis, G. G., & Daniels, R. J. (1995). The role of debt in interactive corporate governance. *California Law Review, 83*(4), 1073–1113. doi:10.2307/3480898

Yeh, S. S. (2011). Ending corruption in Africa through United Nations inspections. *International Affairs, 87*(3), 629–650. doi:10.1111/j.1468-2346.2011.00994.x

ADDITIONAL READING

Brutents, K. N. (1972). *A Historical view of neo-colonialism.* Moscow: Novosti Press.

Daniel, A. (2005). Multinational corporations and the realization of economic, social and cultural rights. *California Western International Law Review, 35,* 53.

Eweje, G. (2006). The role of MNEs in community development initiatives in developing countries corporate social responsibility at work in Nigeria and South Africa. *Business & Society, 45*(2), 93–129. doi:10.1177/0007650305285394

Jagdish, B. (2001). *In defense of globalization.* New York: Oxford University Press.

Kolk, A., & Lenfant, F. (2010). MNC reporting on CSR and conflict in central Africa. *Journal of Business Ethics, 93*(S2), 241–255. doi:10.1007/s10551-009-0271-1

Sedereviciute, K., & Valentin, C. (2011). Towards a more holistic stakeholder analysis approach: Mapping known and undiscovered stakeholders from social media. *Journal of Strategic communication, 5*(4), 221-231.

Chapter 3
Results of Prior Empirical Investigations

INTRODUCTION

This chapter primarily presents some of the previous empirical investigations that have been conducted within the overarching context of *Corporate Social Responsibility* (CSR). The chapter also presents and discusses diagrams on foreign direct investment (FDI) stocks and flows in the period 2005 and 2011. These data form part of the basis for the formulation and testing of at least two consequential null hypotheses. This chapter notes that an increase in foreign direct investment stocks and flows indicate in various regions of Africa increased activities of MNCs in the region. An empirical analysis that involves independent calculations by this researcher is presented in this chapter.

The bivariate correlation analysis focuses on the investigation of the level of associations among three variables, including foreign direct investment stock, flows and labor force in agriculture in two regions of Africa. The results of regression analysis to predict the impact of annual FDI stocks and flows on total annual agriculture labor force in Eastern Africa and Western Africa, respectively, are reported. The two regions were chosen for comparisons because they are among some of the most populous and economically dynamic regions in Africa.

DOI: 10.4018/978-1-5225-2534-9.ch003

DISCUSSION OF EMPIRICAL INVESTIGATIONS

The discussion in the previous chapters reinforced the notion that the discourse of stakeholder theory as it relates to the management of competing stakeholder interests has emerged as a significant theme in the management literature (Pratt, 1991; Harrison & Freeman, 1999; Bhattacharya, Korschun and Sen, 2008). Hence, the literature abounds with examples of empirical investigations to test the validity of stakeholder theory. Several of these studies have been conducted under the broader theme and rubric of CSR. Thus, in a study conducted by Whitehouse (2006) the author concludes that the context within which CSR has been implemented hinders its potential to offer stakeholders a more efficient means of evaluating its impact on corporate performance.

McWilliams and Siegel (2001) tested several hypotheses that the level of CSR will depend on and conclude that there is an ideal level of CSR, which managers can determine through cost-benefit analysis. The authors also conclude that there is a neutral relationship between CSR and a firm's financial performance. Bhattacharya, Korschun and Sen (2008) provide some insights that borrow from the literatures on means-end chains and relationship marketing. The authors further provide a conceptual model that explains how CSR provides stakeholders with numerous benefits including psychological, functional and in the domain of values.

It is also suggested that the type and extent to which stakeholders gain access to these benefits from CSR activities influence the quality of the relationship between them and the company. Ogden and Watson (1999) examined the contention of stakeholder theory that a firm can simultaneously enhance the interests of its shareholders and other relevant stakeholders. The results show that although improving relative customer performance is a costly exercise, shareholder returns respond to a significantly positive manner to such improvements.

Lund-Thomsen (2009) assesses the promises and pitfalls of competing approaches to South African industries and in community mobilizing in environmental governance. The author argues that a multilevel approach is necessary to evaluate the impact of CSR and corporate accountability initiatives. However, it is suggested that both approaches fail to address the underlying global-level structural causes of conflicts between MNCs and stakeholders in developing countries. The author calls for fundamental changes in the global economy in order to resolve conflicts between companies and stakeholders.

Pratt (1991) identifies the challenges that MNCs from developed countries face in sub-Saharan Africa and examines the direct foreign investment and development interests of the region. The author claims that deontological ethics are largely at odds with sub-Saharan African value systems because they emphasize autonomous actions that satisfy individual goals. Hence, both utilitarian and situational ethics are said to be consistent with the region's investment codes, development interests, and value systems. It is suggested that these ethical theories can assist MNCs to meet effectively their social responsibilities to the region.

Pratt's perspectives are consistent with the relational view of the corporation and its stakeholders put forward by Buchholz and Rosenthal (2005). The authors suggest that feminist theory is a way of developing a more relational perspective. But since this perspective lacks a systematically developed conceptual framework for undergirding its own insights, pragmatic philosophy is offered as a way of undergirding this perspective and a relational understanding of the firm and its stakeholders (p. 137-38). These views are also consistent with the ones put forward by Greenfield (2008):

Corporations are collective enterprises, drawing on investments from various stakeholders who contribute to the firm's success. For a business to succeed over time, it must induce people and institutions to invest money, whether in the form of equity or loans. It must induce people to invest their labor, intelligence, skill, and attention by joining the firm as employees or managers. It must induce local communities to invest infrastructure of various kinds. None of these investors—for investors they all are—contributes its input out of altruism or obligation (p. 1043).

Elms, Berman and Wicks (2002) applied a qualitative case study approached in their study of the health care industry to demonstrate that stakeholder theory's focus on ethics may be problematic. The authors claim that the lack of recognition of the effects of incentives in the basic conceptual framework of stakeholder theory limits the theory's ability to explain managerial behavior. The authors suggest that while ethics provides a basis for stakeholder prioritization, incentives influence whether managerial action is consistent with that prioritization. The authors recommend at integrated approach that include both ethics and incentives to increase the explanatory power of stakeholder theory.

One might pose the question "are CSR practices in themselves sufficiently enough to bring about systemic change in the management of labor?" Jones, Marshall and Mitchell (2007) pose this question in a study on two Australian mining companies. The authors conclude that CSR considerations are not sufficiently powerful in themselves to bring about systemic change in the effective management of labor. The authors also conclude that companies may not act consistently in line with their stated CSR commitments (p. 64). That they may in fact, continue with controversial policies if there are perceived sound business reasons for those policies (p. 64).

Chong (2009) reports research findings from a qualitative exploratory study on employee participation in CSR activities and the formation of corporate identity related to DHL's CSR strategy employed in a disaster-response program in the Asia-Pacific region in the wake of the Asian tsunami in 2004. The author observes that close alignment between CSR strategy and corporate identity and internal communication are crucial to the success of CSR programs. Chong also concludes that over time, the interactions between corporate identity and participation in CSR activities form a self-reinforcing loop. The next section takes a critical look at the pattern, distribution and circumstances of foreign direct investment (FDI) flows to Africa.

MULTINATIONAL CORPORATIONS (MNCS) AND FDI FLOWS TO AFRICA

During the 1960s and 1970s, foreign investment and MNCs operating in developing countries including Africa, were regarded as threats to economic development and national sovereignty (Ellis, 1990). In this period international business was on the defensive (p. 2). This was a time when the U.N. Commission on Transnational Corporations (TNCs) and several codes of conduct to regulate the activities of MNCs were launched (p. 2).

But by the end of the 1980s, the situation had dramatically transmogrified. Former communist political regimes, including the former Soviet Union and the Peoples' Republic of China began promulgating new foreign investment laws aimed at attracting foreign capital and technology. Ellis (1990) expanded on this theme by citing the fact that attendees at a UN sponsored-high level

Roundtable on the UN Code of Conduct on TNCs in Montreux, Switzerland in October 1986 unanimously concluded that:

Transnational corporations, in pursuing their economic objectives, can make a contribution to the development process by providing capital, technology, managerial resources and markets (p. 2).

The growth areas for MNC investments in the developing world were East Asia and to some extent Latin America. Cantwell (1997) citing Cantwell (1991) concludes that Africa has been an important investment location of European MNCs. Prominent among these are companies from countries that have had traditional historical ties to African countries, including British and French MNCs, and to a lesser degree German and Italian companies (p.156).

In the 1970s, inward foreign direct investment (FDI) flows to Africa constituted only 17.1 percent of the total flows of FDI to developing countries (p. 156). Africa's share of FDI inflows into developing countries fell to 8.9 percent from 1979-1983 as newly industrialized countries took off in the late 1970s (p.156). Africa restored its share of new FDI stocks to 12.1 percent of inflows into all developing countries from 1981-1990 in the wake of the Latin American debt crisis (p. 156-57). Another source, for example, Boafo-Arthur (2003) states that

Estimates of the African Development Bank (ABD) show that Africa's share of FDI to developing countries over the years has declined from an average 16 percent in the 1970s to 10 percent in the 1980s; and an insignificant 5 percent by the mid-1990s (p.32).

More recent figures of inward FDI flows into specific regions of Africa from 2005-2011 are presented below in figure 1. Meanwhile figure 2 presents existing FDI stocks in Africa from 2005-2011. The data below and other sources (for example, Cantwell, 1997) confirm that much of the investment that has taken place in Africa in more recent years has been highly concentrated in a relatively narrow range of countries. Much of this investment has been concentrated in the northern African region with a notable exception of 2011; where the average investment in the Western African region was higher than other regions (Figure 1).

Most African countries remain oriented toward resource-based activities, which suggest that the position of the continent in the international division of labor has not changed much since the colonial period (Cantwell, 1997).

18

Figure 1. Foreign direct investment flows, annual, 2005-2011 US dollars at current prices and current exchange rates in millions.
Source: UNCTAD, FDI database (www.unctad.org/fdistatistics).

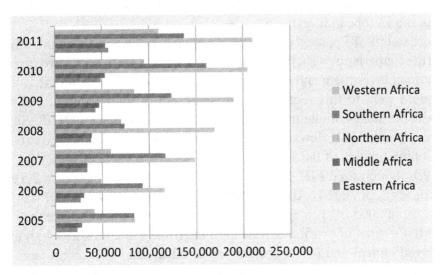

Figure 2. Foreign direct investment stock, annual, 2005-2011 US dollars at current prices and current exchange rates in millions.
Source: UNCTAD, FDI database (www.unctad.org/fdistatistics).

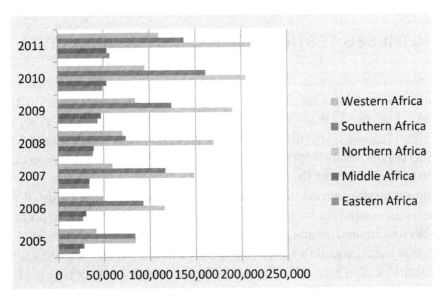

Unlike in the past, investments in Africa today are concentrated more in mining and oil rather than in agricultural plantations (p. 160). Thus, the primary sectors of mining and oil have received the major share of United States and European investment.

For example, 87 percent of French investment and 68 percent of investment from the Netherlands went into the primary sector (p. 160). Forty-two percent of German investment and around 30 percent of investment from the United Kingdom went to this sector as well. In an era of globalization, FDI has become the means of integrating into the global marketplace (UNDP, 2007). However, global FDI flows to Africa have remained small compared to other developing regions of the world.

Even though total FDI inflows to Africa rose to $3.1 billion in 2005, a historic high compared to the 1990s, the region's share in global FDI was just 3 percent in 2005 (p. 12). Subsequent sections of this chapter make the case that MNCs' goal of profit maximization in Africa has conflicted with their perceived ethical and social obligations as advanced by different versions of stakeholder theory. Hence, on the basis of this argument, this researcher puts forward an alternative conceptual framework for critical stakeholder governance in Africa. A crucial plank in this framework is the notion of communicative action articulated in the next chapter. It is suggested that this framework has the potential of reflecting the genuine interests of all stakeholders in an era of globalization and rapid economic and social change.

HYPOTHESES TESTING AND PREDICTIVE ANALYTICS

This researcher suggests that one could conclude intuitively based on a careful examination of the data that there exists a strong correlation ($r = .001$, $p = .943$) between FDI stocks and flows in the period 2005-2011. And, that FDI flows may be a significant predictor of FDI stocks. Thus, a regression analysis conducted by this researcher showed that FDI flows are a significant predictor of FDI stocks ($b = 5.54$, $p = .001$).

The regression results also show that 94.3 percent of the value of FDI stocks is accounted for by FDI flows. As stated above, two null hypotheses have been stipulated for analysis in this chapter. The major goal of conducting these analytical procedures is to gauge the extent to which activities in the agricultural sector, a major sector in African economies, may or may not have been impacted by the activities of MNCs using FDI stocks as a proxy. It is important to note that several factors, including the nature and structure of FDI flows to Africa and the effects of structural adjustment policies (1980s-1990s) in agriculture on the African continent have influence agricultural, social and economic growth and development in Africa (see for example, Oya, 2006). In view of the operation of these variables, this researcher posits that it is only logical to consider the fact that there are a host of forces are work that must be accounted for in producing a comprehensive model. That having been said, the following hypotheses are stipulated for analyses:

$H_{(0)}$: Annual FDI stock has a significant impact during the years 2005-2011 on total annual agricultural labor force in the Eastern African region.

$H_{(01)}$: Annual FDI stock has no impact during the years 2005-2011 on total annual agricultural labor force in the Eastern African region.

$H_{(0)}$: Annual FDI stock has a significant impact during the years 2005-2011 on total annual agricultural labor force in the Western African region.

$H_{(02)}$: Annual FDI stock has a significant impact during the years 2005-2011 on total annual agricultural labor force in the Western African region.

The results of the correlation analysis in Table 1 showed that there was statistically significant relationship between annual FDI stock during the years 2005-2011 and total agricultural labor force in Eastern Africa ($r = .998$, $p = .001$). This suggests that perhaps foreign direct investment stock during the years 2005-2011 correlated ($p<.05$) with increased agricultural labor. The results in the Table 1 also showed there was statistically significant relationship between the balance of payments during the years 2005-2011 and total agricultural labor force in Eastern Africa ($r = -.815$, $p = .025$).

Based on this singular finding, one could deduce therefore that whereas a positive balance of payments of countries in the region could have had a positive effect on the expansion of agricultural activities, a negative balance of payments could have also led to a retrenchment in agricultural activities. Thus, one could also see how this outcome could have resulted in an expansion

Table 1. Correlation Analysis: Continuous predictor variables on Agriculture (EA)

	r	p
Stock	.998	.000**
Balance of payments	-.815	.025*

p<. 05* p<.01**

Table 2. Correlation Analysis: Continuous predictor variables on Agriculture (WA)

	r	p
Stock	-.465	.293
Balance of payments	.488	.317

p<. 05* p<.01**

of the labor force in this sector in the region. On the basis of this finding, this researcher posits that the first null hypothesis was supported and the alternative hypothesis not supported.

Meanwhile, Table 2 showed that there was no statistically significant relationship between annual FDI stock during the years 2005-2011 and the total annual agricultural labor force during the same period (r = -.465, p =.293). The analysis also found that there was no statistically significant relationship between the balance of payments of countries in the Western African region during the years 2005-2011 and the annual agricultural labor force during the same period (r =.488, p =.317). This finding suggests that total annual agricultural labor force during the years 2005-2011 was not sensitive to changes in the balance of payments in the Western African region. This statistical finding demonstrates that the second null hypothesis was not supported and the alternative hypothesis was partially supported.

Results of the stepwise regression analysis are contained in Tables 3 and 4, respectively. In Table 3 for example, the results examined the extent to which the value of total annual agricultural labor force in the Eastern African region during the years 2005-2011 could be predicated from the values of the values of FDI stock and balance of payments, when balance of payments was controlled for in the model. Thus, in this equation, FDI stock (b =.245, p =.000) was a significant predictor of activities in the agricultural sector in terms of total annual agricultural labor in the region. The adjusted R^2 for the model in Table 3 was.996 or 99% and a significant F = 1502.679, p =.000.

Table 3. Results of regression analysis (Eastern African region)

Regression Equation Predicting Agricultural labor force (results of stepwise regression) (N-36)			
Variables	**Coefficient**	**Standard Error**	**p-Value**
Intercept	92209.477	483.312	.000
Stock	.245	.006	.000

R-Square =.997
Adj. R. Square =.996
F statistic = 1502.679
Sig F =.000
p <.05* p <.01**

Table 4. Results of regression analysis (Western African region)

Regression Equation Predicting Agricultural labor force (results of stepwise regression) (N-36)			
Variables	**Coefficient**	**Standard Error**	**p-Value**
Intercept	286161.816	125369.782	.085
Stock	-1.889	1.160	.179
Balance of payments	-3.234	2.414	.251

R-Square =.459
Adj. R. Square =.189
F statistic = 1.698
Sig F =.293
p <.05* p <.01**

Table 4 examined the extent to which the value of total annual agricultural labor force in Western Africa during the years 2005-2011 could be predicted from the values of FDI stock and balance of payments. The results showed that FDI stock (-1.889, p =.179) and balance of payments (b = --3.234, p =.251) were not significant predictors of agricultural activities in terms of total annual agricultural labor force during the years 2005-2011 in the region. The adjusted R^2 for the model in Table 4 was.459 or 45% and a significant F = 1.698, p =.293. One would suggest that readers should consult prior research by Hussain (1999) for further discussion of the balance-of-payments constraint on economic growth rate differences among African and East Asian economies.

THE PATH TO CRITICAL STAKEHOLDER GOVERNANCE IN AFRICA

As stated earlier, the negative effects of globalization in Africa associated with the operations of MNCs could be tempered through mandated corporate compliance with the rules of the road. It is suggested that a strong and enlightened African state is required to facilitate this process. A strong and enlightened African state is called for because with the advent of globalization and the transition to the neoliberal economic model that currently governs international trade; the African state has become increasingly powerless.

Domestic challenges such as the lack of transparency, rampant corruption, structural weakness, and political instability have occasioned the diminishing stature of the African state and its retreat from an interventionist role in economic affairs. In the face of these challenges, Africa has been compelled thanks to the pressures of globalization, to compete at the global level with dwindling institutional capacity and other material resources (Boafo-Arthur, 2003). Thus, Boafo-Arthur reinforces these views when the author states that

Even if the relevance of the earlier phases of globalization is discounted, one can assert that the nature of the current global interconnectedness of different peoples and societies occasioned by the sheer magnitude of technological development has drawn Africa into the vortex of the global economy as never before. Thus, Africa finds itself as a partner, albeit a weak one, in the global political economy (p.30).

What is at stake here for successful governance is creating policy spaces that increase the bargaining power of African states in their dealings with MNCs. This is crucial because the very nature of state-firm bargaining has changed in light of globalization and the neoliberal economic model. As the consequences of the economic reforms and the liberalization of foreign investment rules of the 1980s and 1990s, the modern state has been redefined to assume a weaker position. For MNCs, the extraction of maximum profits had become a primary preoccupation at the expense of other factors. These processes have had implications in terms of the bargaining power of the state (Haslam, 2007).

Thus, whereas in the past the state, particularly in developing countries, attempted to channel private investment to serve its developmental objectives, the scenario has changed as MNCs have become more powerful. (p. 1167). This changed situation and in light of the stiff competition for FDI to African countries, some countries like Ghana sought to enact policies such as the Ghana Investment Promotion Act (GIPC).

The GIPC was enacted in 1994. The GIPC accords preferential treatment to foreign investors that Ghana did not even reserve for Ghanaians. Only a few activities are reserve for Ghanaians under GIPC. These include petty trading, operation of taxi-fleet services of less than 10, pool betting, lotteries, beauty salons and barber shops (UNDP, 2007). Ghana does not impose performance and local content requirements on foreign firms; thereby weakening its bargaining position considerably (p. 107).

Other countries in West Africa like Liberia, has recently signed several concession agreements with MNCs in the mining and agricultural sectors that have left much to be desired. In their article *An Institutional Analysis of Corporate Social Responsibility in Kenya*, Muthuri and Gilbert (2011) concluded that attention must be paid to factors that hamper CSR uptake such as government regulations and government capacity to enforce commitment to regulation. The authors also urged the formation of a vibrant civil society that promotes civil regulation of MNCs. Elaborating on the evolution and nature of states' bargaining power in developing countries, Haslam (2007) notes that

Through bargaining the state attempted to channel private investment to serve its own developmental objectives. It was also argued that the bargain 'obsolesced' over time to the benefit of the state, which was able to make increasing demands on the investor once the investment was in place. Thus, in state-firm bargaining, the state was generally viewed as the stronger party over time (p.1167).

In an effort to curb 'regulatory actions' by governments, MNCs have increasingly sought to strike agreements where minimum standards for investment protection and the codification of investor-state dispute settlement provisions, which allow foreign firms to sue governments for expropriation (p.1169). These and other external and internal constraints that limit the state's ability to act to protect the interests of African countries and stakeholders increase the stakes for an enhanced stakeholder approach to corporate governance.

An enhanced stakeholder approach to corporate governance that incorporates the interests of all relevant stakeholders is strengthened when African governments develop the necessary institutional capacity to tackle the issue of corruption. Commenting on some of the worst cases of corruption in Africa, Mcferson (2009) states

The answer lies in the extreme corruption in these countries, where most of the revenue from extractive industries has been and continues to be appropriated by unaccountable ruling elites. In fact, it is precisely this large revenue that allows the elite to buy control, keep the security apparatus happy, repress moves toward political participation, and preclude a minimally decent distribution of resources—a syndrome known as the resource curse. (p. 1529).

Yeh (2011) in a recent article on the issue of corruption in Africa reminded us that the International Monetary Fund (IMF) and the World Bank have traced poor economic performance in Africa to misguided dirigisme, such as central planning and command economic prescriptions. However, Yeh (p. 630) agrees with other African political economists that the core problem is uncontrolled corruption--the abuse of power for personal gain—rather than dirigisme. But I would argue that the problem of African underdevelopment and state failure is multifaceted--a combination of uncontrolled corruption and a host of other internal and external factors, including the current terms of economic globalization.

The issue of human rights and the working and environmental conditions of workers and countries in which MNCs operate have featured prominently in the literature on stakeholder theory and the ethical responsibilities of firms generally (Monshipouri, Welch and Kennedy, 2003). Thus, Monshipouri, Welch and Kennedy (2003) have indicated that codes of conduct are not enough to promote the human rights of workers employed by MNCs.

Hence, voluntary codes of conduct are viewed as public relations tools that are not for the benefit of workers because they can never be expected to be enforced (p. 979). It is suggested that states and international bodies should be expected to protect the rights of workers "...by regulating companies through both national and international legislation." (p. 979). And one would further suggest these national and supranational entities should also ensure that there are capable institutions to enforce relevant legislation.

This suggestion supports the case for stronger enforcement mechanism under the aegis of the state and other international arrangements. Through these means, an ethical landscape and normative framework that protects the interests of African stakeholders, particularly those who are marginalized could be created. The United Nations and its Global Compact has been cited as an important avenue to compelled compliance by MNCs with their presumed ethical responsibilities to host communities (p. 981). Aaron (2012) using the case of the activities of oil companies in Nigeria's delta region, called for new models of corporate-community engagements in response to the shortcomings of the old models by oil MNCs.

The Global Compact has emphasized the corporate social responsibility of MNCs in terms of their protection of human rights and contributions to the vitality of host communities (p. 981). Other issues, such as sustainable development, assumed greater urgency in 2002 when the United Nations World Summit on Sustainable Development (WSSD) brought the issue of sustainable governance onto the global agenda. Elkington (2006) predicts that the focus of future waves of global engagements on issues of sustainable development will emphasize themes like creativity, breakthrough innovation and entrepreneurial solutions to great challenges like pandemics and climate change.

Porter and Linde (1995) posited that properly designed environmental solutions can trigger innovations that decrease the total cost of a product or improve its value. It is suggested that these types of innovations would allow companies to use a range of inputs more productively and judiciously, such as raw materials, energy and labor. The efforts and institutional designs being initiated at the global level to affect corporate behavior are necessary but by no means sufficient. As Monshipouri, Welch and Kennedy (2003) remind us

The mere adoption of a code of conduct is only the first step in a long process. international law has to protect these rights by holding corporations liable if they do not comply with universally accepted human rights standards, such as those outline in the Global Compact. By focusing solely on the economic effects of the MNCs, international law has yet to hold these companies accountable for the social effects they have on developing countries (p.982).

Other critics of globalization and MNCs have advocated for an international court envisioned as a system outside the United Nations (p. 985). The South Commission has advocated preference for regional integration and new controls over MNCs through regulation of foreign investment. Others have floated the idea of linking the International labor Organization's rights-based approach with the enforcement and sanctioning functions of the World Trade Organization to address the labor rights of workers when they come under assault by MNCs (p. 985).

Carbonnier, Brugger and Krause (2011) have alluded to the fact that market incentives and regulation offer a plausible avenue to bring about decisive change in the behavior of elites in producer states as well as MNCs. The authors refer to the Kimberly process, whose success it is alleged resulted from concerns over the risk of a consumer boycott of diamonds (p. 260). Readers would note that detailed information on the Kimberly process Certification Scheme for diamond trade (KPCS) and other transparency measures in Africa, such as the Extractive Industries Transparency Initiative (EITI) can be found in an article by Carbonnier, Brugger and Krause (2011). Thus, an enhanced stakeholder theory justifies punitive social regulation when MNCs fail to undertake socially responsible actions in fostering environmental protection and the human rights of their employees (Stark, 1993; Aaron, 2012).

On the basis of the aforementioned discussion, it is suggested that a conceptual model of critical stakeholder approach could help temper some of the negative effects of globalization on the economic and social development of African countries. The model is presented in the next chapter and it is predicated upon the normative presuppositions of stakeholder theory (Hendry, 2001; Freeman, 2005). It also takes into consideration an enhanced role for a rehabilitated African state free of the current constraints of uncontrolled corruption and working in conjunction with appropriate international entities. Rehabilitated African states shall become enlightened states. This suggests that these states shall become aware of their interests and know how to protect those interests in their dealings with MNCs in an increasingly globalizing world. This they shall do by allow the growth of a deliberative ethics based on the rules of discourse outlined in the chapter four.

CONCLUSION

The dawn of the 21st century has been profoundly impacted by the social, political, and economic forces of globalization. Globalization has increased the gulf between rich and poor countries in terms of levels of income growth and socio-economic development. Economic and structural inequalities within countries have also increased as a result of globalization. In this chapter, this researcher argued that globalization has had a negative impact on African countries and that these consequences should be addressed through an enhanced stakeholder approach to corporate governance.

The chapter called for greater coordination between companies, international bodies and African states to more adequately address the negative effects of globalization. The chapter also upholds the notion that the task of African states, when corporate self-regulation fails, is to play a crucial role in tempering the negative effects of globalization. Such task could be executed through appropriate social regulation and the implementation of enforceable mandates by African states and other relevant institutions.

The chapter held that the deepest form of globalization appropriately describes the nature of the activities of MNCs in Africa countries. This researcher suggests that governance infrastructures have lagged far behind the rapid pace of globalization thus resulting in problems, challenges and conflicts. Thus, this researcher would suggest that to resolve these issues, new governance structures should be set into motion to properly and more effectively govern the interconnections between countries that globalization has intensified. Normative stakeholder theory envisages an enabling environment for corporate governance in which all stakeholders, including host communities and the African state can thrive.

This chapter argued that a critical stakeholder approach to the ethical and social responsibilities of firms has the potential of altering some of the negative effects of globalization in terms of the activities of MNCs in African countries. Hence, this researcher puts forward a model, which is predicated upon the normative presuppositions of stakeholder theory as crystallized in the work of other authors. The model also takes into consideration an enhanced role for a rehabilitated African state free of the current constraints of uncontrolled corruption and the trappings of hegemonic discourse and power. These perspectives are fully developed in chapter four.

REFERENCES

Aaron, K. K. (2012). New corporate social responsibility models for oil companies in Nigeria's delta region: What challenges for sustainability? *Progress in Development Studies, 12*(4), 259–273. doi:10.1177/146499341201200401

Bhattacharya, C. B., Korschun, D., & Sen, S. (2008). Strengthening stakeholder-company relationships through mutually beneficial corporate social responsibility initiatives. *Journal of Business Ethics, 85*(2), 257–272.

Boafo-Arthur, K. (2003). Tackling Africa's developmental dilemmas: Is globalization the Answer? *Journal of Third World Studies, 20*(1), 27–54.

Buchholz, R. A., & Rosenthal, S. B. (2005). Toward a contemporary conceptual framework for stakeholder theory. *Journal of Business Ethics, 58*(1-3), 137–138. doi:10.1007/s10551-005-1393-8

Cantwell, J. (1991). Foreign multinationals and industrial development in Africa. In P. J. Buckley & L. J. Clegg (Eds.), *Multinational Enterprises in Less Developed Countries.* London: Macmillan. doi:10.1007/978-1-349-11699-7_9

Cantwell, J. (1997). Globalization and development in Africa. In J.H. Dunning & K.A. Hamdani, K.A. (Eds.), The new globalism and developing countries (pp. 155-179). Tokyo: United Nations Press.

Elkington, J. (2006). Governance for sustainability. *Corporate Governance: An International Review, 14*(6), 522–529. doi:10.1111/j.1467-8683.2006.00527.x

Ellis, C. N. (1990). Foreign direct investment and international capital flows to Third World Nations: United States policy considerations. In C. D. Wallace et al. (Eds.), *Foreign direct investment in the 1990s: A new climate in the third world.* Dordrecht: Martinus Nijoff Publishers.

Elms, H., Berman, S., & Wicks, C. A. (2002). Ethics and incentives: An evaluation and development of stakeholder theory in the health care industry. *Business Ethics Quarterly, 12*(4), 413–432. doi:10.2307/3857993 PMID:12708454

Freeman, E. (2005). A stakeholder theory of the modern corporation. In L. P. Hartman (Ed.), *Perspectives in business ethics* (3rd ed., pp. 112–122). Boston: McGraw-Hill Irwin.

Greenfield, K. (2008). Stakeholder theory and the relationships between host communities and corporations. *Case Western Reserve Law Review, 58*(4), 1043–1065.

Haslam, P. A. (2007). The firm rules: Multinational corporations, policy space and neoliberalism. *Third World Quarterly, 28*(6), 1167–1183. doi:10.1080/01436590701507594

Hendry, J. (2001). Missing the target: Normative stakeholder theory and the corporate governance debate. *Business Ethics Quarterly*, *11*(1), 159–176. doi:10.2307/3857875

Hussain, M. N. (1999). *The balance-of-payments constraint and growth rate differences among African and East Asian economies*. Oxford, UK: African Development Bank.

Jones, M., Marshall, S., & Mitchell, R. (2007). Corporate social responsibility and the management of labour in two Austrian mining industry. *Corporate Governance International Review*, *15*(1), 57–67.

Lund-Thomsen, P. (2009). Corporate accountability in South Africa: The role of community mobilizing in environmental governance. *International Affairs*, *81*(3), 619–633. doi:10.1111/j.1468-2346.2005.00472.x

McWilliams, A., & Siegel, D. (2001). Corporate social responsibility: A theory of the firm perspective. *Academy of Management Review*, *26*(1), 117–127.

Muthuri, J. N., & Gilbert, V. J. (2010). An institutional analysis of corporate social responsibility in Kenya. *Journal of Business Ethics*, *98*(3), 467–483. doi:10.1007/s10551-010-0588-9

Ogden, S., & Watson, R. (1999). Corporate performance and stakeholder management: Balancing shareholder and customer interests in the U.K. privatized water industry. *Academy of Management Journal*, *42*(5), 526–538. doi:10.2307/256974

Oya, C. (2006). From state dirigisme to liberalism in Senegal: Four decades of agricultural policy shifts and continuities. *European Journal of Development Research*, *18*(2), 203–234. doi:10.1080/09578810600708163

Porter, M. E., & Linde, V. D. C. (1995). Green and competitive: Ending the stalemate. *Harvard Business Review*, *73*(5), 120–139.

Pratt, C. B. (1991). Multinational corporate social policy process for ethical responsibility in sub-Saharan Africa. *Journal of Business Ethics*, *10*(7), 527–541. doi:10.1007/BF00383351

Stark, A. (1993). What's the matter with business ethics? *Harvard Business Review*, *71*(3), 38–48. PMID:10126154

UNCTAD. (2012). Inward and outward foreign direct investment flows, annual, 1970-2011. Retrieved from http://unctadstat.unctad.org/ReportFolders/

UNCTAD. (2012). Inward and outward foreign direct investment stock, annual, 1980-2011. Retrieved from http://unctadstat.unctad.org/ReportFolders/

UNDP. (2007). *Asian foreign direct investment in Africa: Toward a new era of cooperation among developing countries*. New York: United Nations.

Whitehouse, L. (2006). Corporate social responsibility: Views from the frontline. *Journal of Business Ethics, 63*(3), 279–296. doi:10.1007/s10551-005-3243-0

Yeh, S. S. (2011). Ending corruption in Africa through United Nations inspections. *International Affairs, 87*(3), 629–650. doi:10.1111/j.1468-2346.2011.00994.x

ADDITIONAL READING

Frynas, G. (2005). The false developmental promise of corporate social responsibility: Evidence of multinational oil companies. *International Affairs, 81*(3), 581–598. doi:10.1111/j.1468-2346.2005.00470.x

Gray, L. C. (2008). *Hanging by a thread: Cotton, globalization, and poverty in Africa*. Ohio: Ohio University Press.

Kieh, G. K. (2008). *Africa and the new globalization*. Aldershot: Routledge.

Matwijkiw, A., & Matwijkiw, B. (2009). From business management to human rights: The adoption of stakeholder theory. *Journal of the Indiana Academy of the Social Sciences, 13*, 46–59.

Pamela, G., & Tsikata, D. (2010). *Land tenure, gender and globalization: Research and analysis from Africa, Asia and Latin America*. New Delhi: International Development Research Center.

Taylor, S. D. (2012). *Globalization and the culture of business in Africa: From patrimonialism to profit*. Bloomington: Indiana University Press.

Wonkeryor, E. L. (2016). Globalization and its implications for Africa. New Jersey: Africana Homestead Legacy Publishers.

Chapter 4
A Moral Framework for Business Communication and Collaboration

INTRODUCTION

This chapter posits that an ethic of collaboration manifested through the principle of discourse ethics can contribute to the search for norms of appropriateness and the good. It is suggested that these norms of appropriateness are adjunct to models of development that contrast with anti-developmental norms such as political and cultural hegemony, the lack of fairness, corruption and fraud. Other anti-developmental practices to enumerate here include the abuse of child labor, governance and sustainability, and the environment.

Yet, others include the nefarious activities of some MNCs in Africa. However, why this researcher hopes that an ethic of collaboration might temper some of the current challenges of globalization, one should note that the sum total of any sustained and conscious effort at reform must be a resultant of serious considerations of internal processes concerned with the lifeworld and system (Reed, 1990; Scherer and Palazzo, 2007). Proceeding from these premises, the chapter upholds the view that moral and ethical codes of conduct in business and society are essential for sustainable economic growth and business development in Africa and elsewhere.

These statements are also apropos to the nature and character of transactional relationships in Africa; an area that has been designated as underdeveloped on a multitude of economic and social indices. Research findings in the business

DOI: 10.4018/978-1-5225-2534-9.ch004

ethics literature demonstrate that where ethical considerations and moral forms of life are absent, business development and societies have suffered and hence remained chronically underdeveloped. Mulinge and Nesetedi (1998) affirmed this perspective in their article on corruption and colonialism in sub-Saharan Africa.

Subsequent sections of this chapter examine definition of the problem and other relevant issues. The chapter also considers a discussion of discourse ethics in terms of how it constitutes the philosophical foundation and a primary theoretical source of an integrative business ethics approach---based on the collaboration hypothesis. The chapter suggests that an integrative collaboration hypothesis constitutes a viable ethical platform for business practice. It further holds that the integrative features of the collaboration hypothesis make it a viable moral framework to guide organizational practice and change in Africa. Finally, the chapter concludes with a presentation of final thoughts by underscoring the need to explore future opportunities that advance diverse research agendas and possibilities in the field.

DEFINITION OF THE PROBLEM

As noted in the previous chapter, foreign direct investment (FDI) from overseas concessions in Africa has performed miserably due primarily to a variety of factors, including corruption, graft, and other institutional paralyses. Meanwhile, in specific African countries such as Nigeria, the largest economy in Africa, corruption in both the private and public sectors remains historically and legendarily endemic. Many concerned citizens and news commentators, including the former Governor of The Central Bank of Nigeria, Sanusi (Nossiter, 2014; Kay, Bala-Gbogbo and Mbachu, 2014) claimed just few years ago, that billions of United States dollars went missing from the petroleum sector, depriving the Nigerian economy of needed injection of financial resources to meet the country's manifold development needs.

South Africa, with all its enormous potential, has also not fared very well in terms of the perversion of transactional business relationships on account of many recorded infractions of ethical rules of business conduct. Other countries in sub-Saharan Africa are also reported to have been affected by the corrosive effect of corruption on business development and the growth of viable corporate and individual entrepreneurialism (Mulinge and Nesetedi,

1998). Basically, both small and large firms have underperformed miserably because of the lack of a moral framework for effective collaborative endeavors. These claims are supported by assertions made in the 2015 report filed by Transparency International—a premier agency for research on corruption in Africa and elsewhere.

There are other reasons for failure to note, of course. Given these social and ethical perversions, business ethics scholars and social scientists have preoccupied themselves with generating adequate explanatory models that fit the problems (see for example, Reed, 1990; Mulinge and Nesetedi, 1998; Scherer and Palazzo, 2007). Others (Meisenbach, 2006; Ferrell 2011; Garcia, Marza, 2012), working in the field of moral philosophy, have foregrounded categories of social and philosophical theory such as non-instrumental rationality and the primacy of emancipatory goals.

This chapter, and in fact, the entire book should feature among such efforts. The chapter posits that a process of sustained organizational and even structural change could be unleashed through a critical approach to business ethics and communication. Toward this end the chapter proposes that the collaboration hypothesis is a viable candidate for a business ethics and communication approach. The collaboration hypothesis is built on critical stakeholder principles and it examines modalities of positive collaboration that leads to organizational success. The collaboration hypothesis is also being presented here in the contexts of Ubuntu—an African philosophical tradition and mode of cultural practice—and a moderate communitarian perspective—also embedded in African social and cultural norms.

DISCOURSE ETHICS AND BUSINESS COMMUNICATION

Agreeing with Moon (1995), one would posit that the search for the ultimate foundation for moral and political beliefs led social theorists to the concept of discourse as a moral foundation for defending the legitimacy of social practices. This quest also inevitably led to the introduction of discourse theory in explaining communicative practices in varying fields of human endeavors including education, business ethics, moral and political theory. Thus, the political theory of discourse ethics privileges the value of social communication and rational discourse in the adjudication of claims by all those who have stakes in the operations of a firm or other organizational forms. Discourse ethics is both method and mode of procedural justification of action-oriented norms. This approach in the overarching philosophical theory of modernity was given rise to through the publication of the Theory of Communicative Action in 1981 (Borradori, 2003).

This publication by Jungen Habermas signaled a turn toward a new framework of inquiry that integrated a variety of theoretical sources including the ordinary language school of J.L. Austin and John Searle. Other influences on this new framework at that time came from Norm Chomsky generative approach to linguistics, the psychological and moral theories of Jean Piaget and Lawrence Kolhberg, and the social model of analysis elaborated by George Herbert Meade and Talcott Parsons (p.66). In terms of sociological sources, one would add that perhaps it was Parsons' theory of social action that was one of Habermas's influences.

Discourse ethics presupposes that the basic question as to which way to proceed in determining a fit between the immediate profit motive of firms and he long-term welfare of ordinary citizens and stakeholders must be decided upon through discursive processes of legitimation and participatory models of development. Through these processes, one would suggest that the likelihood that people would become empowered and motivated is enhanced.

Hence, what is at stake here ultimately is to curb the normative exercise of power (Ingram, 1987). One should concede that this form of exercising power, invariably leads to groupthink and the ossification of bureaucratic and antidemocratic rules into norms that militate against the presuppositions of practical discourse in our justification activities. Indeed, this form of exercising power ultimately leads to dogmas, philosophical foundationalism thus foreclosing possibilities for reason's critique. Furthermore, one should look no harder to observe that normative exercise of power also presents itself permanently in structures of distorted communication (p. 13).

Taking his cues from the German philosopher Fichte, Habermas accepts the principal thesis "that in emancipatory reflection, our practical interest in becoming free, universal moral agents coincides with our theoretical interest in gaining knowledge about the natural and social conditions that shape us." (p. 13). This suggests that an emancipatory praxis that embraces discourse ethics could become a medium of validating competing validity claims in the operations of firms and perhaps macro-constitutional entities.

The methodology of discourse ethics and the universalization principle "U" are superior abstract notions of freedom because of their inherent moral constraints imposed on our justification activities. One would argue here that through discourse ethics, participants or agents are able to arrive at a consensual agreement about an issue at hand (like the question of how to curb corruption, for example), or at least arrive at some sort of mutual understanding of each other's viewpoints and epistemological situations.

Hence, such a dialogic and learning process is inherent in the very nature of moral and ethical discussions in organizations. Moon (1995) has suggested that Habermas's conception of communicative or discourse ethics is in a way more ambitious than the moral theory put forward by the philosopher John Rawls. The author further suggested that Habermas sought to establish the moral constraints that Rawls takes for granted (p. 145). Moral arguments according to Habermas should not be made in the form of deduction, they must be made in the form of argumentation analogues to the principle of induction for empirical questions. This principle he refers to as the principle of universalization ("U") (p. 149). In this light, every valid norm is expected to fulfill the condition that

All affected can accept the consequences and the side effects its general observance can be anticipated to have for the satisfaction of everyone's interests (and these consequences are preferred to those of known alternative possibilities for regulation) (p. 149).

In fact, one should note here that the universalization principle (U) in general was captured by Robert Alexy's rules or symmetry conditions (Kelly, 2000, pp. 229-43). Hence, these rules presupposed that the formal features of rational argumentation under the universalization principle ("U") (p. 149) must include the following presuppositions:

1. Every subject with the competence to speak and act is allowed to take part in a discourse.
2. Everyone is allowed to question any assertion whatever.
3. Everyone is allowed to introduce any assertion whatever into the discourse.
4. Everyone is allowed to express his attitudes, desires, and needs.
5. No speaker may be prevented, by internal or external coercion, from exercising his rights as laid down above.

The above presuppositions add up to the view that a contested norm cannot meet with the consent of the participants in a practical discourse if the principle of universalization ("U") is not satisfied. In fact, Arash Abizabeth (2005) recognizing this point has cited Habermas thus

Only those norms proposed that express a common interest of all affected can win justified assent. To this extent, discursively justified norms bring to expression simultaneously both insight into what is equally in the interest of all and the general will that has absorbed into itself, without repression, the will of all (p. 204).

Abizabeth (2005) further intimated that Habermas introduced his principle of universalization ("U") as a response to Kant's categorical imperative. Murphy (1994, p. 115) paraphrasing Habermas, indicated that the principle of 'U' redefines what is moral thus suggesting that moral questions are those that can be debated rationally.

Abizabeth (2005) claimed that Habermas's discourse ethics applied to what has been termed morally justified norms of action, which means it applies to rules "that specify whether an action is morally obligatory, permissible, or forbidden." Rasmussen (1990) alluded to the fact that the aim of discourse ethics was to produce a consensus, which assumes a certain kind of symmetry and reciprocity defined by an equal opportunity to make wishes and feelings known

Discourse ethics may be said to provide a procedural justification for truth and validity claims. When one speaks of something being valid, one assumes a certain background consensus presupposing comprehensibility, truth, correctness or appropriateness, truthfullness or authenticity... (p. 64).

Irish Marion Young (1994) has noted that Habermas shares with John Rawls and other moral theorists

The idea that moral dialogue requires people to adopt a standpoint of impartiality toward all particular experiences and to assent to only those principles and judgements that are consistent with that impartial standpoint (p. 166).

Benhabib (p. 166) expands on this notion of impartiality by adopting Hannah Arendt's interpretation of Kant's construct of "enlarged thought." According to Benhabib, the "enlarged thought" of moral judgment requires one to imaginatively represent to herself the perspectives of others in a moral discourse (p. 166).

The construct of "enlarged thought" also requires for its successful exercise the ability to take the standpoint of the other... The more perspectives we are able to present to ourselves, all the more we are likely to appreciate the possible act-descriptions through which others will identify deeds. Finally, the more we are able to think from the perspective of others, all the more we can make vivid to ourselves the narrative histories of others involved (Cited in Young, 1994, p. 166)

However, I should note that Iris Marion Young and other writers have theorized that the concepts of reversibility and the Hegelian reciprocal recognition embedded in the idea of impartiality are contested categories, to say the least. Young (p. 169) for example, notes that it obscures difference and wrongly presupposes a reversibility of moral standpoints. Abizabeh argued that like R. M. Hare's moral theory, Habermas's discourse ethics is a two-level moral theory (2005, p. 197). He also agreed with Shelly Kegan that all moral theories can be analyzed into the factoral and foundational levels (p. 197).

The principle of universalization ("U") or discourse ethics is perceived as operating at the foundational level, not factoral level. The reason for this assumption is that a factoral theory seeks to justify actions, whereas a foundational theory seeks to justify norms of action. Abizabeh thus suggests that:

An action is right just in case it conforms to a justified norm appropriately applied. Obviously, then, the primary evaluative focal point of Habermas's foundational theory is moral norms. Practical discourses of justification do not seek to justify actions entirely but seek to justify norms of action, according to which actions are in turn morally evaluated (p. 198).

Elaborating extensively on the central principle of universalization as a foundational theory, Abizabeth further notes:

And the substance of his factoral theory is deontological in Kegan's sense: On Habermas's view, an action is right (whether morally permitted or required) just in case it is permitted or required by a justified norm... the question is, of course, how norms are to be justified, and here we come to the foundational level of Habermas's theory. It is at this second, foundational level Habermas introduces the principle of universalization ("U") (p. 198).

Habermas (Murphy III, 1994, p. 116) has posited that the principle of 'U' "acts like a knife that makes razor sharp cuts between evaluative statements and normative ones, or between the good and the just." This sentiment is elaborated further upon in the following passage:

Habermas believes that the moral principle "U" through its requirements that all concerned must accept the consequences and side effects for everyone's interests that a proposed norm's universal observance can be anticipated to have provided the best means for distinguishing evaluative questions (those questions which cannot be resolved consensually) from moral questions... "U" can only work, however, through the engagement of participants in an actual practical discourse. The need for actual discourse reflects Habermas's belief that the formal nature of "U" (and the subsequently derived "D") requires the content derived from an actual context be introduced before any moral conclusions can be drawn (p. 116).

Some authors, including Seyla Benhabib, reject Habermas's core idea of discourse ethics and the universalization principle that for a norm to be valid all affected participants must freely accept the consequences and side effects "that the general observance of a controversial norm can be expected to have for the satisfaction of the interests of each individual" (Moon, 1995, p. 154). Both Benhabib and Agnes Heller (p. 112) have focused part of their criticism of Habermas on his distinction between the just and the good in the context of the reconstruction of social democracy.

These criticisms notwithstanding, the challenge of business ethics and moral philosophers in Africa is to generate hypotheses that fit both the constraints suggested by Habermas's pragmatic theory and the finest traditions in indigenous social and cultural norms. This is the theoretical challenge that the collaboration hypothesis attempts to meet. African scholars must learn to operationalize these ideal constructs not merely as a reflection of already existing social facts but as conceptual frameworks for critical analyses. The specific Habermasian features of the collaboration hypothesis assume---as Garcia-Marza has indicated in paraphrasing Habermas that "negotiations, compromises, and agreements that demand moral validity also arise within most civil institutions, including small and large firms." (emphasis added). The next section examines these issues.

COLLABORATION, ETHICS, AND ORGANIZATIONAL CHANGE

The collaboration hypothesis is a framework for moral action and organizational change. It is essentially undergirded by the collaboration curve and the acceleration principle. The collaboration curve depicts the acceleration of the forces and factors of production that define organizational performance in a profit-maximizing context. It is based on a hypothesis, which posits that the performance of firms is directly proportional (*ceteris paribus*) to the degree of stakeholder participation in the social and strategic decisions of firms.

Jones (1995) for his part claimed that cooperativeness and trustworthiness can lead to a significant competitive advantage. While collaboration theory is ubiquitous in social psychology (Levine & Moreland, 2004), it is yet to gain root in the fields of management and business communication. This paper is a humble attempt to fill some of this void. Indeed, it is an attempt to provide an interpretation of moral theory that has salience in the context of organizational development. Hence, the collaboration curve has been put forward as explaining a phenomenon that exists as a form of linear relationship between two central variables: that encompass the communication and normative function and the efficiency function—suggesting both the procedural justification of norms and efficiency of the productive process. The collaboration curve is also a product of a careful discernment of aspects of micro foundations, critical stakeholder theory, and discourse ethics. It provides an understanding that posits symmetry between aspects of critical stakeholder theory, such as the impartial adjudication of alternative claims and the normative framework of discourse ethics.

These sources, in effect, undergird the theoretical foundations of the collaboration curve and its corresponding hypothetical assumptions. As briefly noted above, one should further note that the collaboration curve is built on a teleological ethical doctrine (in contrast to Kantian deontology) that subscribes to an ideal state of human interaction through rational speech. In this context, it signals a shift that is synonymous with Habermas's reading of Kant as aptly noted by Borradori (2003):

In Habermas's reading these conditions limit Kant's conception of the public sphere within monological boundaries. Monologism refers to the idea that the individual's participation in the public sphere is limited to the simple sharing of her already constituted opinions and moral decisions. In the monological perspective, moral reasoning is defined as a hypothetical conversation with oneself (or with an imaginary listener) (p. 59).

The collaboration hypothesis is further a natural reflection of the African experience. And it can also form a platform for understanding reciprocity, convergent and divergent thinking, learning and other factors that constitute the dynamics of a firm's performance (Levine & Moreland, 2005, p. 166). Thus, the Ghanaian philosopher Kwame Gyekye (1988), viewed the individual within the African setting as possessing of both a communal sensibility and a concept of self and volition. He describes the African social order as amphibious, manifesting features of both community and individuality.

In a subsequent work titled: *Tradition and modernity: Philosophical reflections on the African experience*, Kwame Gyekye (1997) reinforced this moderate communitarian stance, which gives due recognition to individuality. What the author is doing in putting forward this view is attempting to come to terms with both the natural sociality and individuality of the human person (p. 41). In this metaphysical construal, Gyekye (p. 41) impresses upon the reader possibilities for integration of individual desires and social ideals and demands.

Senghor (1963) somewhat echoed these views in the 1960s; when he regarded traditional society as a society where the group could have priority over the individual without crushing him. Senghor suggested that through dialogue and reciprocity, the individual could blossom within the framework of group and communal solidarity. These philosophical precepts are reinforced by the principle of Ubuntu, which emphasizes a communal ethic. Ubuntu is an African philosophical belief that states that 'I am because we are', a belief also rooted in collectivist aspirations and approaches embedded in African culture and organizational practice (Nkomo & Kriek, 2011, p. 462). Thus, Ubuntu, like language, also speaks to the very essence of our humanity. In furtherance of this perspective, Mbiti (Lassiter, 1999) posits that the individual lacks latitude for self-determination outside the context of the traditional African family and community. This is how Mbiti (ibid) describes this collectivist and collaborative viewpoint:

Whatever happens to the individual happens to the whole group, and whatever happens to the whole group happens to the individual. The individual can only say: "I am, because we are; and since we are, therefore I am." This is a cardinal point in the understanding of the African view of man. (p. 4)

The premises of Ubuntu in conjunction with a moderate communitarian perspective (as put forward by Gyekye) also form one of the pillars of the collaboration hypothesis. Furthermore, these assumptions are somewhat consistent with Alfred Aldler's psychological dispositions. Adler, the founder of individual psychology, proposed to avoid the reductionism and determinism of Sigmund Freud by putting forward an overarching theory of social interest (Rich & Devitis, 1985). Adler described egocentric strivings as neurotic and thus counter-productive to his value system. Consequently, he embraced cooperation as a prime motive force.

Adler viewed cooperation as a "necessary invention in man's evolution." (p. 25). Thus, Adler provides some albeit unsystematic psychological basis of the morality of collaboration and its epistemological underpinnings. As Angioli and Kruger (2015) have noted

Adler's vision of the destiny of mankind arose from his sense of the fundamental inter-relatedness of people in community and the challenges each member of the human community faces in constructing the story of his or her life in a holistic and purposive manner. The discourse of Adlerian psychology was a product of the intersection of German philosophy, social and political context, and the psychologies of the Viennese physicians and psychotherapists whom Adler counted as colleagues (p. 237)

The collaboration hypothesis and its curve amplify a normative perspective and also satisfy the requirements of individual and group motivation that leads to efficiency in terms of micro performance of firms; and the actualization of emancipatory interests. This paper proposes, on the basis of the workings of the collaboration hypothesis, that where there is an absence of motivation due to participants feeling a sense of alienation, a breakdown of trust between management and workers might ensue. Such a breakdown of trust between stakeholders might also be a result of distortions in communication among other factors, caused by various species of strategic action (Young, 1990). Kelly (2000) has contrasted communicative action with strategic action. The author defined strategic actions as actions oriented toward success influenced by egocentric aims. Meanwhile, communicative actions involved actions in which agents are oriented toward reaching understanding (p. 226).

Young (1990) has indicated that in strategic action illocutions are used as a means to an end other than reaching understanding about normative claims regarding right conduct (p. 106). This is so because the activities of a business organization—by its very nature—demands a cooperative process in a situation, which could best be described as one of apparently unstable balance (Garcia-Marza, 2012). This view captured by Garcia-Marza (2012) is presented as follows:

From the perspective of this set of expectations, the company clearly appears as a permanently unstable balance of different interests with a clear difference in the capacities and opportunities available to satisfy these interest (p. 107).

This researcher submits here that this disequilibrium process could be tempered by explicit moral commitments that derive from a process of procedural justification and the presuppositions of reasoned discourse. Readers should examine the diagram below to see how the collaboration and consensual validation of substantive norms affects other factors relative to the economic and social performance of firms; and ultimately the communities in which they operate.

That these variables might be linked in various magnitudes have been confirmed to some extent by several recent empirical studies (see for example, Jane, 2005; Chiu and Sharfman, 2011). Indeed, Jane (2005) reports that collaboration and change management are stronger influences of organizational effectiveness, than for example, management procedures and board performance. Other scholars (Hogg, 1994), working in the field of social psychology, including Levine and Moreland (2004) sought to

Figure 1. Performance, collaboration and the theory of justification

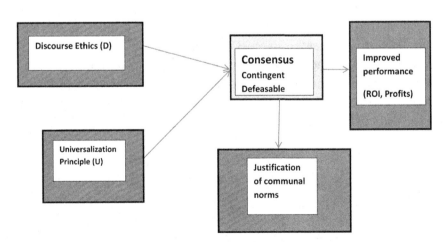

analyze the social processes of group cohesiveness, creativity and scientific collaboration. Levine and Moreland underscored the critical role played in collaboration by shared cognition and group problem solving in their reference to Ferrell's (2011) definition of collaboration circles:

A collaboration circle is a primary group consisting of peers who share similar occupational goals and who, through long periods of dialogue and collaboration, negotiate a common vision that guides their work. The vision consists of a shared set of assumptions about their discipline, including who constitutes good work, how to work, what subjects are worth working on, and how to think about them... For a group of scientists, it might be a new theoretical paradigm. Each member comes to play an informal role in the circle, and each role may have a history as the group develops over time. Even while working alone, the individual members are affected by the group and the roles they play in it (p. 165).

Ferrell's aforementioned description may also apply to collaboration among group members and work teams in a variety of contexts. In a much recent work by Chun, Sandoval and Arens (2011, p. 190) the authors listed the benefits of collaboration between the public and the government. What the collaboration hypothesis presented in this paper demonstrates is that forms of variable collaboration in firms can lead to increased organizational performance.

The accentuation of deliberative and discursive principles can mark a process of acceleration that ensures that performance attains its highest potential. On the basis of this conclusion, one could suggest intuitively that processes of organizational collaboration are a reaffirmation of the acceleration principle. One should note here that this process of intersubjective legitimation of norms and productive efficiency may very well be distinct from the imperatives of technical and bureaucratic rationality. Indeed, in their critique of bureaucratic rationality and method, Max Horheimer and Theodor W. Adorno (2002) made the critical observation

Technology is the essence of this knowledge. It aims to produce neither concepts nor images, nor the joy of understanding, but method, exploitation of the labor of others, capital. What human beings seek to learn from nature is how to use it to dominate wholly both it and human beings. Nothing else counts. Ruthless toward itself, the Enlightenment has eradicated that last remnant of its own self-awareness (p. 2).

The aforementioned analyses describe the process of organizational growth on the basis of collaboration in accordance with normative stakeholder principles. This paper therefore holds that the operational assumptions of the collaboration hypothesis presented above are consistent with some of the basic assumptions of normative stakeholder theory (Moon, 1995; Reed, 1999; Borradori, 2003). These include talk of ensuring broad based participation in deciding rules that adjudicate normative claims and evaluative empirical questions. It might also include deciding rules and outcomes on the basis of what is just and therefore what maximizes utility (Appiah, 2003). Hence, when the collaboration hypothesis is written as a linear differential equation, such an equation would assume a standard bracketed form such as:

$$L[y(t)] = f(t)$$

Or

$$\{L\{y(c)\} = f(c)\} \text{ where:}$$

L = linear operator

$Y(C)$ = function of collaboration

F = source term.

The collaboration hypothesis is further consistent with Fleming's (2008) assumptions that the empirical studies of firms can lead to a profit-sacrificing, bounded rational model. The concept of bounded rationality speaks to the intractable problems that natural decision makers faced and the finite computational resources available for making decisions. On the other hand, a profit sacrificing model attaches importance to profits but the stockholder does not receive all the profits, as other stakeholders are considered and appropriately rewarded.

This underlines the importance of corporate governance structures, practices and norms that lead to greater concerns for multiple stakeholders, including those at the lowest rumps of the economic ladder. Analyses of data generated during my doctoral dissertation research in Firestone between the end of 2009 and early 2010 reinforced these presuppositions by pointing toward the following propositions (Johnson, 2010, p. 84):

- Acknowledging the interests of stakeholders is perceived as paramount to soliciting their cooperation in the execution of corporate social responsibility strategies.
- The empowerment of stakeholders by Firestone in terms of the role they play in decision-making is deemed as important to forging a collaborative spirit that benefits all parties.
- The stakeholders should not be alienated from the Liberian government and its institutions as this can cause misunderstanding and economic and social conflict.

The collaboration curve and the hypothesis, which it signifies, presuppose that stakeholders can engage in discourse as a means of developing a moral framework for action-oriented norms. All participants or agents involved in this process can accept the consequences of this process on the basis of the universalization principle ("U") as stipulated earlier.

This paper claims also that the principle of reciprocity and democratic accountability embedded in free expression and rationally motivated practical discourse of this kind in moments of historical transition can foster collaboration and enhance organizational performance. I would submit here, on the strength of the aforementioned analyses, that reciprocity and accountability; that form the essential pillars of discourse ethics might also be enlisted as armories in the fight against corruption, distorted communication, and the hegemonic use of power and privilege in sub-Saharan Africa.

One would submit, on the basis of the above thesis, that the collaboration hypothesis and its counter-hegemonic features present an effective antidote that curbs some of the excesses of the ideology of pure managerial capitalism. This is a form of capitalism that puts the interest of stockholders over those of stakeholders (Reed, 1990). It is also an ideology devoid of an explicit moral commitment. Hence, the collaboration hypothesis, due to its embrace of community and the principles of individual and collective empowerment through discourse ethics, makes it a viable platform for refashioning the philosophy of management in sub-Saharan Africa in the modern epoch. It is also a modest attempt to contribute to the literature through the application of nonmarket solutions.

EXPERIMENTATION AND HYPOTHESIS TESTING

In specific experimental conditions, one would suggest that the collaboration hypothesis could be tested through the application of causal forecasting models using multiple regression statistical techniques (Collier and Evans, 2015). Perhaps and more appropriately, Data Envelopment Analysis could also be used. Data Envelopment Analysis (DEA) is a linear programming based technique for evaluating the performance of administrative (decision) units. Examples of these unites include schools, libraries, banks, university departments, police states, industrial units etc. The advantage of DEA over ratio analysis or regression techniques is that the approach can handle multiple inputs and multiple outputs at the same time. Under the DEA approach, the performance of a decision unit can be evaluated by comparing the best performing units of a sample of administrative units (see Jahantighi et al, 2015).

CONCLUSION

The views expressed in this chapter reinforced one principal notion. And that is the fact that the voices of stakeholders should be heard in regulating interpersonal affairs and conflicts in the context of the operations of firms and other organizational forms. Hence, the chapter upheld the view that the basic question as to which way to proceed in determining a proper fit between the profit motive of firms and the long-term welfare of ordinary citizens must be decided upon through discursive processes of legitimation. One of the objectives of this exercise was to demonstrate how the collaboration curve---and the hypothesis it depicts---forms a basis for understanding some of the most critical aspects of the empirical activities of firms. And that is the nature of organizational collaboration and its statistically normative effect.

It is suggested that collaboration through objective rational discourse can amplify a positive feedback loop akin to double loop learning and consistent with the desire to ensure technical efficiency and adherence to ethical norms and standards of right conduct. Organizational collaboration of the kind discussed in this paper could expand the concept of quality to include social quality. It could also play a more vibrant role in public policy models that foster the development of local communities. Further, it could be used as means of cultivating the reputational capital of small and large firms.

Collaboration—on the basis of discourse ethics—might result in the furtherance of social democratic ethos that sways society away from the problematics of Scylla and Charybdis—in terms of facing the twin pitfalls of the excesses of pure managerial capitalism and the death of possibilities for social transformation. However, one should note that the tentative natures of the views posited here suggest that the collaboration hypothesis and its operational assumptions require further empirical testing. Hence, the chapter acknowledged the need to advance these discussions through additional research. The chapter also proposed several analytic and evaluative tools that could be used in furtherance of such research programs and agendas.

REFERENCES

Abizabeth, A. (2005). In defense of the universalization principle in discourse ethics. *The Philosophic Forum, 36*(2), 193-207.

Angioli, A., & Kruger, P. (2015). A geneology of ideas in Alfred Adlers psychology. *Journal of Individual Psychology, 71*(3), 236–252. doi:10.1353/jip.2015.0028

Appiah, K. (2003). *Thinking it through: An introduction to contemporary philosophy.* Oxford: Oxford University Press.

Bolatito, L. A. (2008). The crisis of leadership in Nigeria and the imperative of a virtue ethics. Philosophia Africana, 11(2), 117-140.

Borradori, C. (2003). *Philosophy in a time of terror: Discussions with Jugen Habermas and Jacques Derrida.* Cambridge: The University of Chicago Press.

Chiu, S.-C., & Sharfman, M. (2011). Legitimacy, visibility, and the antecedents of corporate social performance: An investigation of the instrumental perspective. *Journal of Management, 37*(6), 1558–1585. doi:10.1177/0149206309347958

Chun, S. A., Sandoval, R., & Arens, Y. (2011). Public engagement and government collaboration: Theories, strategies and case studies. *The International Journal of Government and Democracy In the Information Age, 16*(3), 189–196.

Collier, D. A., & Evans, J. R. (2015). *Operations Management.* Boston: Cengage Learning.

Davila, D. R. et al.. (2006). *Making innovation work: How to manage it, measure it, and profit from it.* New Jersey: Wharton School Publishing.

Farrell, M. P. (2011). *Collaboration circles: Friendship dynamics and creative work.* Chicago: University of Chicago Press.

Fleming, J. E. (2008). Alternative approaches and assumptions: Comments on Manuel Velasquez. In L. H. Newton & M. M. Ford (Eds.), *Taking sides: Clashing views in business ethics and society* (10th ed.). Boston: McGraw Hill.

Garcia-Marza, D. (2012). Business ethics as applied ethics: A discourse ethics approach. *Ramon LIUII Journal of Applied Ethics, 3*(3), 99–114. doi:10.4103/2013-8393.107302

Gyekye, K. (1988). *The examined life: philosophy and the African experience.* Accra: Ghana University Press.

Gyekye, K. (1997). *Tradition and modernity: Philosophical reflections on the African experience.* Oxford: Oxford University Press. doi:10.1093/acpr of:oso/9780195112252.001.0001

Hogg, M. A. (1992). *The social psychology of group cohesiveness: From attraction to social identity.* London: Harvester Wheatsheaf.

Horkheimer, M., & Adorno, T. W. (2002). *Dialectic of enlightenment: Philosophical fragments.* Stanford: Stanford University Press.

Ingram, D. (1987). *Habermas and the dialectic of reason.* New Haven: Yale University Press.

Jahantighi,., M. (2015). Project selection with limited resources in data envelopment analysis. *International Journal of Industrial Mathematics, 7*(1), 71–76.

Jane, H. (2005). Exploration of collaboration and organizational effectiveness in Denver County human service nonprofit organizations [Doctoral Dissertation]. University of Pittsburg.

Johnson, T. (2010). *A critical examination of Firestone's operations in Liberia: A case study approach.* Bloomington: Author House.

Jones, T. M. (1995). Instrumental stakeholder theory: A synthesis of ethics and economics. *Academy of Management Review, 20*(2), 403–437.

Kay, C., Bala-Gbogbo, E., & Mbachu, D. (2014). Nigerian President's suspects Sanusi after missing oil concerns. Retrieved May 1, 2015. Retrieved from http://www.blooming.com/news/articles/2014-02-20/Nigerian-Central-bank-governor-Sanusi-suspended-by-President

Lassiter, J.E. (1999). African culture and personality: Bad social science, effective social activism, or a call to reinvent ethnology? *African Studies Quarterly*, *3*(2), 1-19.

Levine, J. M., & Moreland, R. L. (2004). Collaboration: The social context of theory development. *Psychology and Social Psychology Review*, *8*(2), 164–172. PMID:15223516

Mbiti, J. (1992). *Introduction to African Religion*. Nairobi: East African Educational Publishers, Ltd.

Meisenbach, R. J. (2006). Habermass discourse ethics and principle of universalization as a moral framework for organizational communication. *Management Communication Quarterly*, *20*(1), 39–62. doi:10.1177/0893318906288277

Moon, J. J. (2002). Essays in empirical analysis of corporate strategy and corporate responsibility [Doctoral dissertation]. University of Pennsylvania.

Mulinge, M. M., & Nesetedi, G. N. (1998). Interrogating our past: Colonialism and corruption in sub-Saharan Africa. *American Journal of Political Science*, *3*(2), 15–28.

Murphy, T. F. III. (1994). Discourse ethics: Moral theory or political ethic? *New German Critique, NGC*, *62*, 111–135.

Nkomo, S. M., & Kriek, D. (2011). Leading organizational change in the new South Africa. *Journal of Organizational and Occupational Psychology*, *84*(3), 453–470. doi:10.1111/j.2044-8325.2011.02020.x

Nossiter, A. (2014). Governor of Nigeria's Central Bank is fired after warning of missing oil revenue. *NY Times*. Retrieved from http://www.nytimes.com/2014/02/21/world/ governor-of-central-bank-is-fired-after-warning-of-missing-oil-revenue.html

Rasmussen, D. M. (1990). *Reading Habermas*. Cambridge, Mass: Basil Blackwell, Inc.

Reed, D. (1999). Stakeholder management theory: A critical theory perspective. *Business Ethics Quarterly*, *9*(3), 453–483. doi:10.2307/3857512

Rich, J. M., & DeVitis, J. L. (1985). *Theories of moral development. Springfield: Charles C. Thomas Publisher. Johnson, T. (2010). A critical examination of Firestone's operations in Liberia: A case study approach.* Bloomington: Author House.

Scherer, A. G., & Palazzo, G. (2007). Toward a political conception of corporate responsibility: Business and society see from a Habermasian perspective. *Academy of Management Review*, *32*(4), 1096–1120. doi:10.5465/AMR.2007.26585837

Young, I. M. (1994). Comments on Seyla Benhabib, Situating the Self. *New German Culture*, *62*(62), 165–172. doi:10.2307/488514

Young, R. (1990). *A critical theory of education: Habermas and our children's future*. New York: Teachers College Press.

ADDITIONAL READING

Finlayson, J. G. (2013). The persistence of normative questions in Habermass theory of communicative action. *Constellations (Oxford, England)*, *20*(4), 518–532. doi:10.1111/1467-8675.12058

Jutten, T. (2013). Habermas and markets. *Constellations (Oxford, England)*, *20*(4), 587–603. doi:10.1111/1467-8675.12055

Kihlstrom, A., & Isreal, J. (2002). Communicative or strategic action- an examination of fundamental issues in the theory of communicative action. *Constellations (Oxford, England)*, *11*(3), 210–218.

Kim, J. (1999). Communication, reason and deliberative democracy. *Journal of Communication*, *49*(2), 137–138. doi:10.1111/j.1460-2466.1999.tb02798.x

Varga, S. (2011). Habermas Species ethics and the limits of formal anthropology. *Critical Horizons*, *12*(1), 71–89. doi:10.1558/crit.v12i1.71

Chapter 5
Summary and Conclusion

SUMMARY AND CONCLUSION

There is little doubt to stress here that the issue of the activities of multinational corporations (MNCs) has assumed a prominent place on the global economic development agenda. The ethical issues that undergird this agenda have also seized development scholars, the politics of international institutions, and public commentators alike. Thus, the central message of this book is the fact one could desribe the activities of MNCs under the rubric of globalization as being both a blessing and a curse. The book posits that a much more portent response to globalization and the contradictions of multinational capital is when African citizens and publics seek to empower themselves to become aware of their own strategic interests. And, by logical extension, to fight vicorously to defend those interests.

This researcher posits that these processes are distinguish by their counter-hegemonic character, the nature of public discourse and the efficacy of civil institutions. This researcher also reechoes the theme elaborating upon in previous chapters that tempering the negative effects of globalization would require a new appreciation of the role of a rehabilitated African state and its functional insitutions. Agreeing with Zalanga (2016, p.89) it is true that African countries have limited capacity to make autonomous policy decisions. However, it is also consistent with empirical facts that disciplined and visionary leadership can make a strong case for development policies that reflect their socio-historical realities, most eminent priorities and peculiarities (p.89). This brings us to the point of considering insights about the genuine nature of globalization and economic change in Africa and other developing countries.

DOI: 10.4018/978-1-5225-2534-9.ch005

Thus, in this concluding chapter, this researcher will attempt to provide some clues to the crucial concern as to whether "globalization has been a race to the bottom or not." This concern and the response to it comes in light of some of the troubling results globalization has led to in Africa and other parts of the developing world. Thus, in response to the above concern, this researcher argues that there are certain features of globalization that make it a race to the bottom for host countries. However, this researcher notes this argument depends on several factors and a host of *apriori* assumptions, including the specific circumstances of the case (Winters, 2013). The argument also depends on the proposition that trade liberalization, which has often defined globalization, does not lead to higher welfare for host countries and abroad (Wade, 2014). These premises having been established, let us now consider the hypothesis that globalization is a "race to the bottom" for many host countries.

"IS GLOBALIZATION A RACE TO THE BOTTOM?"

Higher levels of international trade in developing countries with relatively weaker labor market institutions lead to cutbacks in welfare spending and social security (Ruth, 2008). Labor power becomes a strong factor mediating the effects of economic globalization on social spending (Vyborny and Birdsall, 2013). This suggests that social spending tends to decrease as a developing country's economy opens to international trade and globalization (p.63). These assumptions tend to support the "race to the bottom in host countries" hypothesis.

Thus, Rudra (2008) argued that since labor market institutions in developing countries are weaker than their counterparts in developed countries, such institutions account for higher levels of "race to the bottom" in the former compared to the latter. Another aspect of globalization that has come under increased scrutiny is the practices and investment decisions of MNCs with regards to host countries.

This aspect pertains to the labor rights of workers as corporations seek out countries that have lower labor standards. A "race to the bottom" tends to be anticipated as governments may restrict labor rights to enhance their comparative advantage in providing a pool of low-cost labor to attract foreign direct investment (FDI) (Blanton and Blanton, 2012).

Blanton and Blanton (2012) examined how the linkage between labor rights and FDI varies across investment sectors. Thus, the authors found that labor rights as a variable is positively related to investment in manufacturing sectors. Trade liberalization under the rubric of globalization also affects inter-country inequality. Even if we accept the hypothesis that trade can increase total income, how incomes are distributed within countries is also a consequential matter in terms of evaluating the gains from trade and globalization.

As Winters (2013. p.47) has suggested, how globalization affects inter-country inequality can occur in two ways: either all countries free their trade "but the consequences for national income differ by country, or only some countries do so, which will affect distribution even if all economies respond to liberalization the same way." However, Vyborny and Birdsall (2013) argued unambiguously that free trade can lead to differential increases in incomes for different groups within countries. Thus, it is further suggested that some groups may lose income in absolute terms (p.57). As Vybony and Birsall (2013) further described this process in the context of cross-country comparisons

Across developing countries, trade should, theoretically, increase the income of all those that participate, and especially of those that begin more closed and so can more fully exploit an opening. In reality, however, some---such as China—have grown rapidly while trading more, closing the income gap with the rich world, but many others—particularly in Africa and Latin America—have not (p.63).

The authors (p.57) also claimed that the poor have initially gained more than the rich in the short run as a result of big increases in agricultural exports due to free trade. However, the authors noted this assumption is tempered by the fact that in the past three decades, the tendency in most countries has been in the other direction (p.57).

Hence, the globalization of markets for goods and services has tended to increase inequality as the relatively rich has benefited more than the poor. The authors further argued that the best solution is to find fair and sustainable means to compensate the losses in terms of the poor from major economic shifts that trade liberalization engenders. It is suggested that these policies are needed to foster political support for trade liberalization, "as well as protecting the losers from disastrous declines in consumption." (p.59).

This approach confirms the basic dependency and center-pheriphery thesis and views put forward by other opponents of globalization (Karns and Mingst,

2010, Kieh, 2016). And that argument is that the rules of the global economy should be rewritten to strengthen protection for developing countries, including their workers, small farmers, poor people, and women (p.55).

One evidence in support of these claims has revealed that poor people in poorer countries tend to bear relatively greater costs of adjustment to structural changes in the economy that globalization might instigate (Vyborny and Birdsall, 2013). It is these and other empirical evidence (Wade, 2014, p.320; Enyoung, 2012) that support the argument that globalization and unbridle economic liberalization is a "race to the bottom" for host countries. This researcher summits that the following recommendations would help to underpine the impulses toward new breakthroughs in public policy and business research. Readers will note these themes also reflect conclusions from the previous chapters of this book. These ideas and themes are stipulated as follows:

1. Globalization requires some modification both at the level of business practice and at the level of its various theoretical conceptualizations. A critical stakeholder theory approach, such as one based on the ethic of rational discourse and reciprocity would enhance the overarching normative, strategic, and instrumental considerations that undergird the stakeholder theoretical model.

2. Globalization has increased the gulf between rich and poor countries in terms of levels of income growth and socio-economic development. Economic and structural inequalities within countries have also increased as a result of globalization. Hence, some of the negative effects of globalization could be addressed through an both an enhanced and critical stakeholder approach to corporate governance.

3. This book concludes that organizational collaboration through objective rational discourse can amplify a positive feedback loop akin to double loop learning and consistent with the desire to ensure technical efficiency and adherence to ethical norms and standards of right conduct. Organizational collaboration of the kind discussed in this book could expand the concept of quality to include social quality. It could also play a more vibrant role in constructing public policy models that foster the development of local communities. The researcher suggests also it could be used as means of cultivating the reputational capital and efficacy of indegenuous small and medium-sized firms operating under a global regime of transnational capitalism.

REFERENCES

Blanton, R. G., & Blanton, S. L. (2012). Labor rights and foreign direct investment: Is there a race to the bottom. *International Interactions, 38*(3), 267–294. doi:10.1080/03050629.2012.676496

Enyoung, H. (2012). Globalization, government ideology, and income equality in developing countries. *The Journal of Politics, 74*(2), 541–557. doi:10.1017/S0022381611001757

Karns, M. P., & Mingst, K. A. (2010). *International organizations: The politics and processes of global governance*. Boulder: Lynne Rienner.

Kieh, G. K. (2016). Africa and economic globalization. In E. L. Wonkeryor (Ed.), *Globalization and its implications for Africa*. New Jersey: Africana Homestead Legacy Publishers.

Rudra, N. (2008). *Globalization and the race to the bottom in developing countries: Who really gets hurt?* New York: Cambridge University Press. doi:10.1017/CBO9780511491870

Vyborny, K., & Birdsall, N. (2013). Does free trade promote economic equality? In *Controversies in globalization: Contending approaches to international relations*. Los Angeles: Sage Publications.

Wade, R. H. (2014). Growth, inequality, and poverty: Evidence, arguments, and economists. In J. Ravenhill (Ed.), *Global political economy* (4th ed.). Oxford: Oxford University Press.

Winters, L. A. (2013). Does free trade promote economic equality? In *Controversies in globalization: Contending approaches to international relations*. Los Angeles: Sage Publications.

Zalanga, S. (2016). The postcolonial state: Theoretical insights and lessons on the role of the state in promoting economic development and cultural change. In E. L. Wongeryor (Ed.), *Globalization and its implications in Africa*. New Jersey: Africana Homestead Publishers.

ADDITIONAL READING

Bardhan, P. (2004). The impact of globalization on the poor. In S.M. Collins & C. Graham (Eds.), *Globalization, poverty, and inequality*. Washington, DC: Brookings Institution Press. doi:10.1353/btf.2005.0001

Barro, R. (2000). Inequality and growth in a panel of countries. *Journal of Economic Growth*, *5*(1), 5–32. doi:10.1023/A:1009850119329

Biersteker, T. (2000). Globalization as a mode of thinking in major institutional actors. In N. Woods (Ed.), *The political economy of globalization*. New York: St. Matin's.

Frieden, J. A. (2006). *Global capitalism*. New York: North.

Friedman, T. L. (2000). *The lexus and the olive tree*. New York: Anchor Books.

Held, D., & Mcgrew, A. (2007). *Globalization/Anti-Globalization* (2nd ed.). Cambridge: Polity.

Chapter 6

Cities, MNCs and Globalization: An Annotated Bibliography

INTRODUCTION

This chapter presents an annotated bibliography that encapsulates current trends regarding contending perspectives and theoretical constructs on the spatial and temporal characteristics of cities and MNCs being influenced by globalization. Thus, this postscript also provides an annotated bibliography of current discussions and debates in the extant literature on the link between globalization and the various responses to the phenomenon itself manifested in the literature on global city theory. Global city theory as an intellectual sub-discipline is at once a product of diverse theoretical perspectives rooted in sociology, economics, urban studies and public policy theory. It is suggested that the discourse of global city and globalization has affected specific cities in Africa such as Johannesburg and Accra as much as it has affected cities in other parts of the world. References are made to these cities in some of the studies included in this annotated bibliography (Grant and Nijman, 2002; Buechler, 2002).

Finally, two essays are produced here featuring Mumbai—an emerging global city in the developing world and Chicago—a global city in the developed world. This researcher hopes that these essays will capture some of the spatial and economic contrasts and commonalities and hence concrete empirical groundings of theoretical discussions reflected in articles included

DOI: 10.4018/978-1-5225-2534-9.ch006

in the annotated bibliography. As reflected in previous chapters, today's ethical challenges facing MNCs are difficult to truly understand without an understanding of the dynamics of urbanity and capital mobility as well as the social and economic processes these dynamics have unleashed.

GLOBALIZATION AND GLOBAL CITY THEORY

The eminent global city scholar Saskia Sassen (2010) informs us that the city has become a central strategic site distilling major subjects that confront society. Globalization and the new information technologies are also viewed as being among dominant forces reconfiguring social, economic and political processes (p. 4). This researcher suggests it is these dominant economic and technological forces that have led to the formation of new collectivities, scales and units, such as cities and regions. Thus, the list of articles included in this section speaks to these processes unleashed by globalization and how they have led to an emerging concept of global city. Readers will note MNCs operating under the rubric of globalization have not escaped some of the ethical and social contradictions that are the most distinguishing features of today's global cities.

Sassen, S. (2010). The city: its return as a lens for social theory. *City, Culture and Society, 1*(1), 3-11.

   This article posits that today globalization is producing major changes that have become visible most notably in global cities. The challenges, as posited by Sassen (p. 1), is to produce scholarship and analytic tools that explain these complex and multivalent urban instances to allow these instances to be constructed as objects of study. The author suggests that in fact, urbanization of major processes repositions the city as an object of study in ways that could lead to crystal definitions of what exactly is the city. And this researcher would add that these processes have led to the contemporary discourse of the global city.

Grant, R., & Nijman, J. (2002). Globalization and the corporate geography of cities in the less-developed world. In N. Brenner & R. Keil (Eds.), *The Global Reader*. London: Routledge.

In this study the authors are critical of dominant approaches to global city theory because of their primarily "western bias" and their failure to pay careful attention to studying cities that fall beneath the upper tiers of the global city hierarchy. On the basis of this criticism, Grant and Nijman put forward a new approach to the study of cities in developing countries. Hence, the authors posit a phase-model of urban development that takes into consideration colonial and postcolonial conditions. A number of generalizations reflecting the evolution of urban spatial structures within each phase are proposed. Grant and Nijman present a comparative case study of Mumbai in India and Accra in Ghana, West Africa; two cities located in former British colonies that have undergone significant socio-spatial transformations in the wake of economic liberalization policies since the 1980s. Hence, the analysis in this study focused on the post-1980s phase of globalization, when foreign direct investment increased significantly. Three empirical issues are explored building upon a survey of foreign companies in each city: "the scope of transnational corporate activity, the geographical location patterns of transnational corporate activity, and the relation between transnational corporate location patterns and the urban geographies of domestic firms." (p. 27).

Buechler, S. (2002). Sao Paulo: Outsourcing and downgrading of labor in a globalizing city. In N. Brenner & R. Keil (Eds.), *The Global Reader* (pp. 238-245). London: Routledge.

In this study, Buechler develops an ethnographic analysis of working conditions in the squatter settlements of Sao Paulo. The main thrust of the article is concerned with how economic globalization had led to the transformation of urban labor markets in the city of Sao Paulo. In this sense, one could conclude that the author is concerned with the effects of global city formation in the face of intensifying competition under the weight of economic liberalization of the era of the 1980s. The author interviews workers in squatter settlements of Sao Paulo in order to aptly characterize the everyday experience of engaging in outsourced work. The author gives an overall impression of the macroeconomic factors and spatial shifts that resulted in diminishing working conditions of the poor in the city. In an interview Buechler conducted in 1998 with participants in a union adult education program in the Metropolitan Region of Sao Paulo, the interviewee, Nelba, aptly captured the results of these changes:

I entered into a firm in 1979 and stayed 10 years and today... you do not stay a year, that is, if you enter [at all]. These days everything is contracted [out]. It is by contract through an agency- two months, three and goodbye! You have to leave (p. 239).

Merrilees, B., Miller, D., & Herrington, C. (2013). City branding: a facilitating framework for stressed cities. *Journal of Business Research, 66*(1), 37-44.

The article explores the issues connected to stressed satellite cities branding. The purpose of the study, according to the authors, is to develop the nature of a stressed satellite city brand profile. The study was conducted using a quantitative approach that examines two stressed satellite cities, constructing a unifying stressed satellite cities brand profile. The findings of the study focused on developing a common stressed satellite city brand profile amendable to policies aimed at addressing some of the manifold problems of stressed satellite cities.

Smith, M.P. (2002). The global cities discourse: a return to the master narrative. In N. Brenner & R. Keil (Eds.), *The Global Reader* (pp. 238-245). London: Routledge.

In this article Smith calls for rearticulating the concept of global cities to become spaces in which intense sociocultural interactions take place involving transnational social networks. The author argues that this perspective is capable of transcending the limitations of earlier approaches to global cities research by emphasizing the role of social mobilization from below in the production of globalized urban spaces' (p. 377). Smith argues that various assumptions of the global city thesis, when examined from a different perspective, become more difficult to maintain:

Viewed from our current vantage point, global city assumptions about the systemic coherence of the urban hierarchy, the transterritorial economic convergence of global command and control functions, and the declining significance of the nation-state, are more difficult to maintain than they once were (p. 378).

Drenna, M.P. (1989). Information intensive industries in metropolitan areas of the United States of America. *Environment and Planning*, *21*(12), 1603-1618.

This article captures some of the technological processes taking place in the 1980s when some of the current processes in globalization were taking roots. Thus, the metropolitan geography of information intensive industries in the United States during the period of the 1980s is analyzed. Subsequently, the article identified economic forces which fueled the expansion of information intensive industries. The growth of these economic forces is also measured relative to overall GNP growth. The article further identified employment and other data for twenty-four of the largest metropolitan areas in the United States. The author concluded that this analysis led to a revelation of substantial diversity in the degree of concentration of information intensive industries. The next article examines Friedman's world city hypothesis, which unmistakably undergird much of the early literature on global city theory.

Friedman, J. (1986). The world city hypothesis. *Development and Change*, *17*(1), 69-83.

In this seminar article, Friedman seeks to connect the study of cities to the world economy. The author notes that this new approach sharpened insights into processes of urban change. This insight is also thought to offer a needed spatial perspective on a global 'economy which seems increasingly oblivious to national economies.' (p. 69). The author sees his central purpose in this article as listing and discussing the main thesis that links urbanization processes to global economic forces (p. 69). This thesis he calls 'the world city hypothesis.' The world city hypothesis is about the spatial organization of the international division of labor. At such, the author suggests "it is about the contradictory relations between production in the era of global management and the political determination of territorial interests." (p. 69). It is suggested that it is these contradictory relations that the world city hypothesis describe. There are seven interrelated theses connected to Freidman's global city hypothesis (pp. 70-81). They include the following:

1. The form and extent of a city's integration with the world economy, and the functions assigned to the city in the new spatial division of labor, will be decisive for any structural changes occurring within it.

2. Key cities throughout the world are used by global capital as 'basing points' in the spatial organization and articulation of production and markets. The resulting linkages make it possible to arrange world cities into a complex spatial hierarchy.
3. The global control functions of world cities are directly reflected in the structure and dynamics of their production sectors and employment.
4. World cities are major sites for the concentration and accumulation of international capital.
5. World cities are points of destination for large numbers of both domestic and/or international migrants.
6. World city formation brings into focus the major concentrations of industrial capitalism—among them spatial and class polarization.
7. World city growth generates social costs at rates that tend to exceed the fiscal capacity of the state.

Freitag, B. (2003). Global cities in informational societies. *Diogenes,* *50*(1), 71-82.

The author notes that "if the assumption is correct that cities are the real stage of contemporary society, then they must reflect changes unfolding in society in the passage from the 20th to the 21st century. Freitage further notes that this calls for a new examination of our cities and a fundamental change in the theoretical approach in terms of their origin, functioning, and destiny. In this article, the author examines four classical approaches: Max Weber's typology of cities, Walter Benjamin's studies of Paris, 'the capital of the 19th century' in his *Passagenwerk*, the contributions made by utopian socialism to city planning as a major part of the modernization process, and finally, the Chicago School of Robert Park, Ernest Burgess and Louis Wirth.

Sassen, S. (2005). The global city: introducing a concept. *Brown Journal of World Affairs, 11*(2), 27-32.

The author notes that one of the key properties of the current phase of globalization and modernization is the ascendant of information technologies and the associated increase in the mobility and liquidity of capital. It is suggested that privatization, deregulation, the opening up of national economies to foreign firms, and the growing participation of national economic actors in global markets have largely defined the current transformation of the old inter-state system, within which the key players were national states (p. 27). The author notes that it is within this context that we are witnessing a rescaling of the strategic territories that articulate the new system. The author asserts that the weakening of the national as a spatial unit thanks to privatization and deregulation has led to the ascendance of other units or scales (p. 27). Among these units are the subnational, including cities and regions.

Yella, S. (2006). Dynamics of environmental problems in Mumbai. *Clean Technology Environmental Policy*, 8(3), 182-187.

This article discusses the dynamics of environmental problems in Mumbai city. The article adopts an evolutionary concept to the study of the present-day status of Mumbai, a global city. The article divides the process of the environmental evolution of Mumbai into four types; poverty-related environmental issues, rapid economic growth-related environmental issues and wealthy lifestyle-related environmental issues. The article concludes that the city in its current state has rapid economic development-related environmental problems. Poverty-related environmental issues showed little statistical significance. It was also found that industrialization and urban-related environmental issues coexisted with rapid economic development-related environmental issues. One of the practical benefits of these findings, according to the author, is that they provide the necessary policy inputs to city planners so as to avoid various environmental costs that other cities—in both the developed North and developing South--- have already experienced.

McCann, E.J. (2004). Urban political economy beyond the global city. *Urban Studies*, 41(12), 2315-2333.

This article examines the relationship between urbanization and globalization. Unlike many articles written on this topic, the author attempts to transcend the global city hypothesis that has been the focus of much of contemporary urban research. The aim of the author in this article is essentially to capture the globalization-urbanization nexus through a diverse range of cities, large and small. This effort is further developed through a case study of critical moments in the economic development of Lexington, Kentucky. The author claims this city is like many others that have been overlooked by global city researchers.

Frost, M., & Spence, N. (1993). Global city characteristics and central London's employment. *Urban Studies*, 30(3), 547-558.

As observed in some of the studies listed above, this article reflects some of the processes that took place in the 1980s that led to an intensification of the current phase of the evolution of the global capitalist economy. This article examines the recent developments taking place in London that has led to the evolution of the city into a global city. The article demonstrates that the period of the 1990s saw a considerable increase in the level of specialization in financial and business services within the Central London economy that was congruent with such a process. The author observes that one important and distinguishing characteristic of factors shaping the long-term trend of changes in London were influences based in the commercial property market.

Sassen, S. (2013). When the center no longer holds: cities as frontier zones. *CITIES*, *34*, 67-70.

The author states in this article that the frontier zones are located deep inside our large cities. Thus, Sassen (p. 67) views the large complex city, especially if global, such as New York, Chicago or Los Angeles is seen as the new frontier zones. Actors from different worlds meet here, where it is suggested that there are no rules of engagement. The author sees a segment of firms and professionals as forces that can now move in protected global spaces that are also impenetrable. At the other extremes, however, are the less protected, those who need to justify their claims to entry, whether tourists from particular countries and ethnicities and migrant workers. At the most extreme, are those who are "persecuted for whom the crossing of the border has degraded into an operation marked by the violation of their most basic human rights." (p. 68). The most important work facing policy makers and city governors is how to keep these frontier spaces opened through commerce and through the need for peaceful coexistence.

Neal, Z. (2011). Differentiating centrality and power in the world city network. *Urban Studies*, *48*(13), 2733-2748.

This article challenges the equivalence of centrality and power in the study of global cities. Thus, the author notes that centrality and power have become common foci and frequently serve as tools for describing cities' position or status in the global capitalist system (p. 2733). This assumption is problematic in the vie w of the author. Hence, the author concludes applying the proposed measures in a hypothetical world city that centrality and power are distinct and suggests that world cities should be viewed as arising from multidimensional network positions that describe multiple types: "quintessential world cities that are both central and powerful such as New York and London and others that are central but not powerful such as Washington and Brussels and gateway world cities that are powerful and not central such as Miami and Stockholm." (p. 2733).

Phandke, A (2014). Mumbai metropolitan region: impact of recent urban change on the peri-urban areas of Mumbai. *Urban Studies, 51*(11), 2466-2483.

This author notes that global city regions in least and highly developed countries differ in reality in their visions in terms of reorganizing the urban space (p. 2466). It is suggested that claim can be demonstrated within the context of the special reference to the Mumbai Metropolitan Region (MMR). Planned integration of the MMR in the early 1990s into world system was said to have resulted into a massive breakdown in the indigenous space economy leading to deeper changes in the socioeconomic and political and cultural structures of the Peri-urban areas (p. 2466).

Sassen, S. (1996). Cities and communities in the global economy: rethinking our concepts. *The Behavioral Scientist, 39*(5), 629-636.

The author notes in this article that the urban level and the community level need to be incorporated in the analysis of economic globalization and new information technologies. This process will require transcending the relative powerlessness of the localities confronted with hypermobile capital. The author also notes that a focus on place allows researchers to capture new spatial configurations and place-specific characteristics that economic globalization produces and by which it is in turn shaped (p. 632). It is suggested that focusing on cities and communities allow researchers to turn their attention to articulating the geography of strategic places and other social processes at the global scale as well as to "specify the micro-geographies and politics unfolding within these places." (p. 633).

Sassen, S. (2000). Regulating immigration in a global age: a new policy landscape. *Annals, 570*(1), 65-77.

This article argues globalization has produced transformation in the state and interstate system. This process in turn has produced new constraints and opportunities in the handling of immigration. This becomes evident through a critical examination of three key features of current immigration policy in the United States, and to a variable extent, in other highly developed countries as well (p. 65). It is suggested that these three key features are the handling of immigration as (1) a process autonomous from other processes and policy domains; (2) a unilateral, sovereign matter, and (3) operating in a context where the state is given, not affected by the massive domestic and international transformations that are increasingly reconfiguring states and the interstate system (p. 65). The author argues that immigration policy needs to become sensitive to the following factors; interaction effects, develop multilateral approaches, and factor in the changed character of unilateral sovereign authority (p. 65).

Sassen, S. (2006). *Cities in a world economy* (3ʳᵈ ed.). Thousand Oaks: Sage.

This book demonstrates how some cities- New York, Tokyo, London, Sao Paulo, Hong Kong, Toronto, Miami, and Sydney among others have changed considerably over the years. Sassen posits that these cities have evolved into transnational spaces. They have prospered, and they have come to have more in common with one another than with regional centers in their own nation-states as these have declined in importance over the years. It is suggested that these developments require those interested in the fate of cities to rethink traditionally-held dogmas that hold that cities are mere subunits of their nation-states. The author maintains that these changes require reassessment of the importance of national geography in our social world. It is further suggested that the impact of global processes has radically transformed the social structure of cities such as increasing new patterns of social inequality as the organization of labor, the distribution of earnings and the structure of consumption have all been altered.

Sassen, S. (2010). Reading the city in a global digital age: the limits of topographic representation. *Social and Behavioral Sciences*, 2(5), 7030-7041.

The author notes in this article that over the centuries cities have become the epicenter of the intersection of processes with supra-urban and even intercontinental scalings. It is suggested that what is different today is the intensity, complexity, and global span of these networks, and to the extent to which significant portions of economies are now digitized and can thus travel at great speeds through these networks (p. 7037). The author also notes that what is also new is the growing use of digital networks by "often poor neighborhood organizations to pursue a variety of both intra-and inter-urban political initiatives." (p. 7037). As cities and urban regions are increasingly traversed by non-local, including global circuits, much of what we experience, in the views of the author, become impacted by non-local dynamics or simply emblematic of a localization of global processes (p. 7037).

Samers, M. (2002). Immigration and the global city hypothesis: towards an alternative research agenda. In N. Brenner & R. Keil (Eds.), *The Global Reader* (pp. 384-391). London: Routledge.

The author elaborates five key strategies or propositions for further developing Sassen's work at the intersection of immigration studies and urban research. The problem is according to Samers, there is too much emphasis in global city research on economic globalization as happenstance to cities, and not enough focus on endogenous processes such as the question of "how immigrants themselves structure the labor market of large metropolises." (p. 387). The five strategies or propositions put forward for a renewal of the global city literature include the following:

1. Reassess the relationship between international labor migration and urban labor markets.
2. Reassess the relationship between informal employment and global cities.
3. Evaluate critically the growth of sweatshops and downgraded manufacturing.
4. Match exogenous and endogenous processes in global cities.
5. Rethink polarization and inequality.

Chattopadhyay, S. (2015). Contesting inclusiveness: policies, politics and processes of participatory urban governance in Indian cities. *Progress in Development Studies*, 15(1), 22-36.

This article attempts to understand the inclusion of citizens, actors, stakeholders, the structure of incentives and accountability and service delivery outcomes in the context of participatory forms of urban governance in Indian cities (p. 22). It is suggested that new forms of participatory arrangements have been dominated by the middle classes and or power local leaders. The resultant has been the disempowerment of poorer members of the communities concerned. It is also suggested that patronage politics were engraved in these new forms, where the targeted delivery of services yielded high dividends for the patrons (p. 22). The author concludes that the interplay of all these variables make a strong case for the effective engagement of the excluded and disadvantageous section of people with the policies, politics and processes of participatory governance in Indian cities (pp. 22-23).

Sharma, R.N. (2010). Mega transformation of Mumbai: deepening enclave urbanism. *Sociological Bulletin, 59*(1), 69-91.

This article posits that the neo-liberal market-driven economy under the rubric of globalization has been affecting the economy and people of India in various ways. The author analyzes the process of 'enclave urbanism' in Mumbai and concludes that urban renewal is leading to further segregation of citizens into the elite class, who are settling into well-serviced and gated settlements, and the majority of the poor, who are being driven out from the core parts of cities to the peripheries. The author asserts that the construct of 'enclave urbanism' is an inexorable logic of capital and revival of stagnant developing economies that has been articulated by scholars like Manuel Castells, David Harvey, Saskia Sassen and others.

Widmayer, P. (2000). Transforming a global city for the information society: metropolitan Chicago at the crossroads. *Journal of Urban Technology, 7*(2), 23-42.

The author posits that the convergence of three national and global high-performance networks in Chicago has created an opportunity for the city to emerge as a hub of the information economy as the city was once a hub of the industrial economy. The author maintains that key officials of the city have displayed awareness of the fact that it is vital to define the future infrastructure rather than letting it happen by happenstance. It is suggested that research documents that vision, leadership, and investment is critical to urban transformation. The author argues that the experience of Chicago will inform other regions with similar aspirations.

Olds, K., & Yeung, H. (2011). Pathways to global city formation: a view from the developmental City-State of Singapore. *Review of International Political Economy, 11*(4), 489-521.

This article seeks to offer a constructive critique of the global city discourse. The author claims that this discourse puts too much emphasis on the characteristics of global cities and the processes creating global city. What the discourse leaves out, according to the author, is an emphasis on governance issues and their implications. As a result, it suggested, there remain many unanswered questions about how global cities have come into being and 'what is the role of the state in intentionally devising pathways to global city formation." (p. 489). The author proceeds to offer a different conceptual context that tease out the main contours of three forms of global cities; hyper global cities, emerging global cities, and global city-states. The author contends that these three forms have differential developmental paths. The case of Singapore is drawn upon to analyze the unique and specific nature of the global city-state. The author concludes that this form of global city requires to be "rapidly and constantly reworked with a goal of embedding the city into an extraterritorial terrain of network relations." (p. 489).

Fainstein, S.S. (2012). Inequality in global regions, *The Planning Review*, *37*(144), 20-25.

The article argues that while in many developed countries, business and government leaders of large cities aspire to achieve global-city status; there is no evidence to indicate that the inhabitants of global cities and their surrounding regions fare better than those dwelling in smaller cities. Hence, it is suggested that despite being the wealthiest areas in aggregate in respective nations, global city regions tend to have large and dense groups of very poor people, often living in close proximity and juxtaposition with concentrations of the extraordinarily wealthy. The author adopts the views of Sassen regarding the particular industrial and occupational structure of global cities that produces bifurcated earnings structure that in turn result in an outcome of the "disappearing middle." (p. 20). To reinforce these sentiments, one would also cite Murray (2004) who refers to the spectre of the splintering metropolis in characterizing the urban landscapes in Sao Paulo and Johannesburg.

Brenner, N., & Theodore, N. (2005). Neoliberalism and the urban condition. *City*, *9*(1), 101-107.

This article posits that key conceptual, methodological and empirical issues remain to be explored on the question of the neoliberalization of urban space. One of those issues that had to be explored was the concept of "market rule," its strategic and ideological foundations, institutional manifestations, its contradictions and the various ways in which the concept was being confronted by local citizens and stakeholders.

AN ESSAY ON THE EMERGING GLOBAL CITY OF MUMBAI

Introduction

This essay focuses on the current economic, environmental, cultural and political conditions affecting the emerging global city of Mumbai, India. The essay also draws attention to two most critical and important issues that define the historic transformation of Mumbai from the status of an ordinary city and former British colonial outpost into an emerging global city.

These include economic and spatial challenges that also have cultural dimensions. In this essay, this researcher also posits, on the basis of available evidence that the essential forms of these issues are being constantly reconfigured by the current wave of economic globalization and the various contradictions associated with this phenomenon. In fact, one should hasten to add that like many places around the world the current wave of cultural and economic globalization for example, is not only affecting Mumbai as a gateway city, but cities across India as well (Chalana, 2012).

Further, the essay outlines why and how economic and spatial challenges faced by Mumbai are different than those faced by existing global cities. It is noteworthy that embodied in this difference are some of the dividing lines between established and emerging global cities. Finally, the essay suggests an array of policies and programs that could be positively considered in addressing the two identified problem issues. This policy recommendations section is followed by concluding remarks. The next section will first examine data sources and methods followed by another section, which focuses on statement of the problem and how it has manifested itself in the urban transformation of the city of Mumbai.

Data Sources and Methods

There is no doubt that the cultural, political, economic and environmental issues affecting the city of Mumbai calls out for careful analyses, theoretical deconstruction and solutions. And this essay has attempted to address these issues using a variety of data sources and public policy models. These data sources draw on global city theory in the extent literature as well as official documents and reports on the effects of globalization on cities, and on economic and cultural transformations unfolding in the city of Mumbai in particular. The data sources also draw on at least two models in public policy—group theory and institutionalism (Dye, 1981; Brikland, 2005; Hayes, 2007).

Statement of the Problem

The essential hypothesis of this essay is that there are two most important issues that have come to clearly define the evolution of Mumbai into an emerging global city. This researcher argues that these issues could be broadly defined as being economic and spatial in nature. In effect, these are challenges that have also defined some of the manifold consequences of current globalization. However, this researcher should note and as indicated above, the essay will also shed some light on other issues or conditions that are shaping the current state of Mumbai. These include environmental, cultural, civic, and political conditions.

This researcher agrees with Chalana (2012) when the author states that the current wave of globalization that is shaping the course of economic and social developments in India is not the country's first tryst with global exchange. However, the author also notes that the current wave of globalization is unique in its impacts on design and planning (p. 1). This sentiment is somewhat shared by other authors including Grant and Nijman (2006, p. 226). The central point of Chalana's (p. 1) argument is that previous waves of interaction sometime allowed for a "greater degree of indigenization and hybridization." This relationship it is suggested created parallel forms of indigenous modernity. It is suggested that the current wave of globalization however, tends to devalue similar kinds of interaction between the local and the global (p. 1).

One of the problems that have emerged from this pattern of globalization is that cities across India are allowing their built environment that represents unique cultural preferences to be replaced with ones driven by "the planning ideals of global capitalism with little relation to local context." (p. 1).

Some of the problems associated with capitalist modernity are amplified in Sharma (2010). Thus, the author draws our attention to some of the issues associated with change and transformation of Mumbai under the neo-liberal policy agenda (p. 69). Indeed, as with other examples of urban renewal around the world, Mumbai has experienced demolition and reconstruction of existing housing and commercial structures, utilization of vacant or mill lands for rich commercial hubs. This has led to what Sharma appropriately described as 'enclave urbanism.' (p. 70).

Thus, 'enclave urbanism' has meant the mass relocation of slum settlements from strategic spaces and massive development to facilitate the city's infrastructural renewal (p. 69). As the essential hypothesis of this essay suggests, embedded within these changes are both economic and cultural consequences as some indigenous inhabitants are forced to change their lifestyles. Patterns of livelihoods and economic reproduction have also changed under the impacts of these policies and other variables.

These changes have resulted in displacement for thousands of poor families "and their relocation in far-off suburbs." (p. 70). These observations are consistent with the ones made by Grant and Nijman (2006) when the authors suggested urban forms and land uses are to a greater degree influenced by market forces. These are some of the cultural, political, economic and environmental issues that affect the city of Mumbai and that warrant careful analyses and solutions. And this essay has attempted to address these issues using a variety of data sources.

Mumbai as Emerging Global City

The City of Mumbai, formerly known as Bombay is a gateway city for several reasons. A crucial factor responsible for its gateway status is the fact that the city is an undisputed financial and entertainment capital of India. Mumbai is also capital of the state of Maharashtra (Surjan and Shaw, 2009). With a population of over 19 million inhabitants in its metropolitan area, Mumbai is one of the densest and largest cities in the world (Chalana, 2012). This means that the city is the sixth most populated metropolitan area in the world. Due to an annual growth rate of 2.2 percent this population ranking was projected to rise in 2015 (Surjan and Shaw, 2009, p. 420).

The city has built environments that include both indigenous and colonial districts and other hybrid places that define the city's colonial modernity in a variety of ways (p. 1). Mumbai comprises a metropolitan region that is made out of 3 municipal corporations integrating 16 municipal towns, 7 urban centers and 995 villages (Phadke, 2014). The newest and most prominent business district in Mumbai is Nariman Point. It is reported that this land was reclaimed from the Arabian Sea in the 1950s (Grant and Nijman, 2006). Nariman ranks second in terms of its importance for local companies. The area is also by far the most preferred location for foreign companies (p. 233).

As the unquestioned financial capital of the country, large numbers of domestic and foreign banks are based in Mumbai. Further, there is also the presence of the largest stock exchange as well as huge number of investment firms (p. 234). The financial sector of Mumbai has attracted a huge number of related producer services, such as accounting and consulting. The two main business districts are the Fort and Nariman Point (p. 234).

There are also 40 planning authorities constituted at various levels to facilitate the urban renewal process in Mumbai (p. 2469). The Mumbai Metropolitan Region Development Authority (henceforth the MMRDA) has played an active and critical role in the process of making Mumbai an international financial center (p. 2470). The formation of the MMTDA dates back to the 1960s, when efforts were first made to incorporate the inner periphery of Mumbai into the Mumbai Metropolitan Region (henceforth the MMR).

However, as the thesis of this essay attempts to confirm, efforts at metropolitanisation under the free market model in Mumbai ignored the place-specific challenges of the city because they were strongly influenced by cravings to follow Western-inspired models of urbanization (p. 2470). Various efforts at decentralization, such as the development of planned townships like New Bombay also failed. (p. 2470). Urban transformation is today occurring in India with Mumbai at the epicenter.

Shatkin (2014, p. 1) describes this process as a 'remarkable urban moment' and a historical juncture when the Indian state is retreating from the Nehruvian project of state-sponsored modernist urban transformation. Thus, the current urban moment as dubbed by Shatkin has seen the emergence of various schemes for the creation of special economic zones and the building of new towns. What these urban renewal schemes have done in essence is to empower corporate actors in urban governance (p. 1).

In fact, as already mentioned, a major driver of this transformative process is the liberalization of the Indian economy beginning in the early 1990s. Indeed, since the launching of the current wave of globalization in the 1980s, political, cultural and economic circumstances are being constantly reconfigured in both emerging and established global cities across the world. Thus, drawing inspiration from the work of David Harvey, Sharma (2010, p. 70) makes the following observations regarding the causes and consequences of mega transformation and urban renewal:

1.   The perpetual need to find profitable terrains for capital- surplus production and absorption- shapes the politics of capitalism. Urbanization has played an active role in absorbing the surplus product that capitalists perpetually produce for profits.

2.   In the United States of America it is accepted wisdom that the housing sector was an important stabilizer of the economy. [In the context of Mumbai, it has proved to be a booster to stagnant business and manufacturing since the 1980s.].

3.   This more radical expansion of the urban process has brought with it incredible transformations of lifestyle. Quality of urban life has become a commodity, as has the city itself, in a world where consumerism, tourism, and cultural and knowledge-based industries have become major aspects of the urban political economy.

4.   We increasingly live in divided and conflict-prone areas. The results are indelibly etched on the spatial forms of our cities, which increasingly consist of fortified fragments, gated communities and privatized public spaces kept under constant surveillance.

Economic, Spatial, and Cultural Issues

Like other emerging global cities around the world, urban transformation in Mumbai has had implications for the economic and spatial development of the city. These changes have also shaped processes of integration into transnational networks of production, trade, investment as well as the liberalization of city-building processes (Shatkin, 2014, p. 2). Of all the economic problems facing the poor and slum dwellers in Mumbai, only housing has been taken seriously. This was primarily meant to allow commercial exploitation of the strategic locations occupied by the slums (Phadke, 2014). Because it is estimated that nearly 40-45 percent of the population of Mumbai live in slums in the worst living conditions, it is easy for major slums like Dharavi to get the attention of developers (p. 2472).

The rules and regulations related to land acquisitions have received major amendments with the view of silencing and alright taking away the right to resist (p. 2473). For example, the central government has approved of land transfers in various economic zones, including the ones located in the MMR without seeking a consensus from local farmers. Similarly, the environmental laws are also being relaxed to allow various types of infrastructural development involving various projects—the international airport at Kharghar, towns and high rise blocks throughout the MMR, and the Worli-Bandra Sea Link. Sharma (2010) refers to the presence of a darker side of the construction boom in the city and how it is interwoven with the criminal elements.

Phadke (2014) draws our attention to how elite interests have been legitimized by various critical policies. These include policies related to land development, acquisition and control (p. 2474). The author suggests that the nexus of these forces can also be active in creating conditions in which poor and indigenous groups are forced to give up their land resources at cheaper rates. Local democracy is also undermined in the process when local government bodies are bypassed. In addition to these challenges, it is also recognized that several land scams have become common in the MMR (p. 2474).

An emergent transnational economic system has led to spatial polarization in Mumbai with some places experiencing upscaling with others experiencing downscaling at the same time. Phadke (p. 2474) notes that these economic processes are taking place to facilitate the needs of international capital. Other authors have made similar observations (see for example, Chattopadhyay, 2015; Nijman, 2008). There is no doubt that the position of Mumbai as an emerging global city is accelerating vis-à-vis the global economy. This process may be adversely affecting all the new activities penetrating the region and reconfiguring the "hierarchical repositioning of the inner and outer peripheries of the city" (p. 2474). Paraphrasing D'Monte, Phadke (2014, p. 2474) notes that unprecedented levels of physical displacement and the reshuffling of people, conventional industries and unprofitable economic activities have morphed into a common planning strategy. It is suggested that this displacement is not only limited to people but also life spaces (p. 2474). Like in other emerging and established global cities around the world, the most vulnerable groups in Mumbai are the poor and lower-income groups (Sassen, 2006).

In the region of Mumbai about half the population lives in slums, chawls, and squatter settlements (p. 2475). And huge numbers of these settlements are located along railway tracks and on public land. Under the terms of the Mumbai infrastructure project, various infrastructure projects are taking place, which could affect more than 35,000 households in Mumbai alone (p. 2475). In making sense of these processes, this author would evoke sentiments expressed by Murray (2004, p. 38) that "ordinary cities being incorporated into global circuits of trade and investment leads to widely divergent socio-spatial outcomes."

As already indicated, resistance to the urban regeneration schemes in Mumbai are usually brutally suppressed, "often using police force." (Phadke,

2014, p. 2475). These tensions are only going to increase as various plans are at foot to develop IT and software parks, malls, film and entertainment studios, alternate business hubs and a land bank by acquiring commercially profitable lands in the MMR (p. 2475). The sum of all these activities have led to a decline of production activities and growing housing poverty, in tandem with the takeover by vested elites (Sharma, 2010). Murray (2004) refers to the spectre of the splintering metropolis in characterizing the urban landscapes in Sao Paulo and Johannesburg. A similar metaphor could also be used to appropriately describe the process of urbanization in Mumbai; where radical transformation has brought about the creation of new lifestyles and consumerism for the new rich and privileged sections of the city's population (Sharma, 2010, p. 88).

It is suggested that the new enclave-urbanism has created new forms for spatial use, "which increasingly consist of fortified fragments, gated communities and privatized public spaces kept under constant surveillance." (Cited in Sharma, 2010, p. 88). Sassen (2006, p. 74) argues that the space constituted by the world wide grid of global cities has led to "transmigration of cultural forms and the reterritorization of local subcultures". This researcher agrees with her that the question is whether this has created a space for a new politics that goes beyond the politics of identity and culture (p. 74). Indeed, a new politics driven by imperatives linked to participatory governance (Zerah, 2009) essentially geared at the reclamation of rights by the poor in the public sphere along lines suggested by other authors (see for example, Dye, 1981; Heysse, 2006).

Policy Solutions and Recommendations

The policy solutions this researcher proposes here reflect broader political, economic, cultural and environmental trends unfolding in Mumbai. They could also have bearings on the effective management of the city in terms of leading to a much stronger framework for a system of decentralized governance that transcends elite interests to also reflect the interests of the poor. Thus, this researcher would suggest that city and state authorities in Mumbai take critical steps needed to ensure that urban renewal is not just an agenda for speculation and profiteering (Sharma, 2010). There is no doubt that when the poor becomes empowered participants in governance and institutional processes (Dye, 1981), practices such as the capturing of valuable land from low-income populations would be discouraged. Inflation in the housing market has caused considerable pain for the middle-class even more so for the poor of the slums. Instead of a manipulative approach by government in tackling housing poverty, there should be a humane approach to resettlement and rehabilitation (p. 88).

International development organizations, such as the World Bank and other international non-governmental organizations should become a part of such humane, participatory and transparent process of resettlement of affected families. This researcher further proposes that the state should also do more to reinforce the particularistic claims of the poor majority rooted in the politics of identity. This thesis is consistent with the views of Shatkin (2014). The author notes that such attempts present a strong force that has held its own in urban politics in the face of state planning mandates and the domination of global capital. The major test of these normative standards is the extent to which they accentuate the agency of those who are currently excluded from the fruits of economic and social development in the urban renewal and globalization process.

CONCLUSION

This essay presented an account of the current economic, environmental, cultural and political conditions affecting the emerging global city of Mumbai in India. The essay posited that there are two most important issues that define the historic transformation of Mumbai from the status of an ordinary city into an emerging global city. These include economic, spatial and cultural issues. The essay also posited that the essential forms of these issues are being constantly reconfigured by the current wave of economic globalization and the various contradictions associated with this phenomenon. Finally, the essay recommended certain policies and programs that could potentially meet basic normative standards and thus play a crucial role in addressing the two identified problem issues.

AN ESSAY ON THE GLOBAL CITY OF CHICAGO

Introduction

In this essay the characteristics of metropolitan Chicago's global city status are analyzed. This analysis is anchored on a central proposition that proactive policies at the municipal and state levels are essential to maintaining metropolitan Chicago's global city status. This researcher describes the character of these policies and argues that they should seek to shape and address challenges associated with the execution of metropolitan Chicago's global city functions in the context of globalization in the following domains: technology, urbanization, and migration. This researcher will expand on this argument from regional, provincial, national and international perspectives.

The Impact of Globalization and Technology

Chicago is a major city not only in the Midwestern United Sates, but in the country and the world. For example, Chicago is the third largest city in the United States. In the global cities index of 2014, Kearney (2014) placed metropolitan Chicago among the top twenty cities in the world. According to this survey, the metropolitan city of Chicago also ranks among the six leading cities in the Americas, sharing place with New York, Los Angeles, Washington, Toronto, and Buenos Aires. Chicago arose from its humble origins as an old industrial city to achieve the heights of global city status in an epoch of globalization (Widmayer, 2000). Like the case of other global cities, one would argue that in many ways some of these changes have also reflected important transformations in the world economy (Freitag, 2003).

The city has more than seven million citizens spread over a six-county region. The position of the city has been enhanced through its extensive transportation network. Added to this is the location of the busiest airport in the world— O'Hare International Airport. The city today is a hub for so many activities in the technology fields, such as telecommunications, technology development, transportation, financial markets, healthcare, and other sectors (p. 23). The city is also the site of the headquarters of many corporations operating across the most diverse business, research and financial activities. Corporations that are headquartered in Chicago include the following: Motorola, Abott Labs, Baxter, Kraft, Anderson Consulting, AON, the Chicago

Mercantile Exchange, the Chicago board of Trade, Sears, Tellabs, Genuity, Banks, and others that have their home in Chicago (p. 23).

The city is a national center for high-performance digital networking (p. 23). In fact, the presence of high-performance international research and education networks from Canada, Europe, Asia Pacific region, Australia, and Israel are connected to The National Science Foundation's Science, Technology and Research Transit Access Point (STAR TAP). Metropolitan Chicago is also home to the Metropolitan Research and Education Network (MREN) (p. 23). In a small way one could argue that it is part of the reality of globalization that has forced global cities and states to learn how to be more multilateral. Indeed, the multilateralism of states and global cities has assumed many facets affecting trade, city to city partnerships and the handling of global financial crises (Sassen, 2000). And Chicago is no exception to this assumption.

The Metropolitan Research and Education Network was founded by three universities and independent research institutions, including Northwestern University, the University of Chicago, the University of Illinois-Chicago, Fermilab, and Argonne National Laboratory. Private companies such as Ameritech and others collaborated in the founding of this network. Widmayer (p. 25) posits that the network aimed to support an array of advanced applications and to accelerate the development of the next generation Internet and networking technologies.

These networks exist in metropolitan Chicago but they have to be leveraged to help the city maintain its economic, social and political position in this century. This is why this researcher posits that proactive and effective policies will be needed at both micro and macro constitutional levels to maintain the city's global city status. Thus, without these assertive and proactive policies, such as providing the proper incentives for universities and telecommunications companies in the private sector to continue to collaborate, it would be impossible to continue to merge the research objectives of universities and other research institutions in the region and the profit motives of these companies. More than ten years ago, there were frantic efforts in the Chicago region to focus on the best combination of strategies for moving into e-commerce. These efforts included but not limited to the five following objectives (Widmayer, 2000, p. 29):

1. Producing new products and services for the information economy
2. Creating a promotional platform for product marketing and information

3.   Directing product and services distribution and creating distributor networks
4.   Connecting to customers to offer improved quality of service
5.   Facilitating internal management.

In the meantime and given the presence of command and control functions (Sassen, 2006), this researcher should note that it is no coincidence that Chicago satisfies the foundational requirements of global city status (Drennan, 1988; Freitag, 2003). For, headquarters of firms that operate in more than one country are based in metropolitan Chicago (Friedmann, 1986). Further, the city is a key site for "advanced telecommunications facilities necessary for the implementation and management of global economic operations." (p. 78). In addition, because of its dominant position in world's trading futures, Chicago became one of the specialized markets in which the phenomenal growth in levels of financial activity in the 1980s took place (Sassen, 2006, p. 132).

Paraphrasing the work of Saskia Sassen in terms of a description of the essential characteristics of global cities, Freitag also notes that

They provide the full infrastructure needed by the world economy for the realization of international transactions. This includes good airports, hotels, telecommunications, Media, Internet, banking, security, stock exchange, and so on (p. 79).

Urbanization, Migration and Social Fragmentation

This researcher would adopt a dual perspective in understanding urbanization and the distinctiveness of the various socio-economic sectors of Chicago. This perspective emphasizes topographical representations of the city in terms of differences between poor and rich neighborhoods, between commercial and manufacturing districts, transport systems, water and sewage pipes etc. (Sassen, 2001). This researcher proposes that this approach be blended with the effects of economic restructuring that have occurred in the city in the context of globalization (p. 7030).

The effects of economic restructuring and social and cultural dynamics have led to various forms of interconnections among parts of the city. For example, the fact that "a growing share of advanced economic sectors also employ significant numbers of very low-wage workers and subcontract to firms that do not look like those that belong in the advanced corporate sector" reinforces the idea of interconnections between diverse social and residential poles in the city.

In Chicago, like in other global cities in the developed world, expensive residential areas can be connected with poorer ones based on the new demand for low-wage household workers, cleaners, nannies and nurses and nursing assistants, including both native born and migrants to the city from poorer countries around the globe.

This researcher himself does travel to the downtown area, where he teaches. The researcher knows relatives and multitude of friends and family members that have engaged in nursing assistant work in the homecare industry in Chicago and in other cities throughout the United States. Every morning, buses filled with commuters travel from various economically-deprived sections of the city to enter the loop—the site of downtown residential and commercial offices for work as clerks, security workers, cleaners, nursing assistants, traffic wardens, sanitation workers etc.

These multiple interconnections among various parts of the city suggest that mere topographic representations of the city are necessary but insufficient in creating a much comprehensive representation about urbanization, economic change, and spatial fragmentation in the city. The inescapable assertion to make here also is that the city is host to difference and interconnections. It is home to the juxtapositions of fractured communities and gentrified residential neighborhoods. Short (2006) indicates that difference is a vital indicator of the urban experience. This researcher would add that this difference has become accentuated in the face of pressures brought about by globalization and rapid economic and structural change beginning several decades ago.

The sources of difference, as Short (p. 9) suggests, may also include age, ethnicity, socio-economic status, gender etc. Hence, this researcher would note that an overarching imagery of the modern Global City, such as the city of Chicago is the dialectic of sameness and radical difference. This dialectic reflects the contradictions of social polarization conditioned by the transition from an industrial to services based economy. Even before these changes, metropolitan Chicago had always been a city of contrast and radical difference.

This notion was captured much elegantly in the segregation studies of urban sociologists like Park, Burgess and McKenzie (Freitage, 2003). Burgess (p. 75), for example, drew a model of Chicago in which he referred to five different inner concentric loops, starting with a central zoon and a second loop. The second loop contained the underworld, the ghetto, Chinatown, Little Italy, slums, and rooming-houses, and others. There was also a third loop and a fourth loop reflected in this model.

The fourth loop included the residential zone, hotels, the so-called bright light area, apartment houses, and single family dwellings. In my estimation, there is a world of difference between the contemporary Chicago ghetto, such as the gang-infested and economically fractured African-American ghetto communities (mainly on the southwest side of the city) and the Hispanic ghetto (on the Northwest side of the city) and Burgess' fourth loop.

If proactive social and economic policies and empowerment strategies of the types envisaged in this essay could change anything to maintain Chicago's global city status, these are the areas that would have to be fundamentally transformed. Ultimately and as already indicated, strong and effective partnerships among policy actors at the municipal and state levels need to be formed to address some of the corrosive effects of endemic and persistent gang related violence in parts of the city.

On the issue of migration, it is noteworthy that Chicago has one of the richest immigration histories among cities in the United States (Paral, 2015). Immigration has played a pivotal demographic role in metropolitan Chicago. Immigration has added a certain richness and depth to the already diverse economic processes that define global city functions in the case of Chicago. It also accounted for about three quarters of all population growth in the 1990s (p. 2). Between 2000 and 2002, immigration added 113,000 persons to Cook County (home to Chicago) during period when the county experienced net out-migration of the native born.

Paral (p. 4) reports that census data indicate that the economic conditions of immigrants improved during the 1990s in metropolitan Chicago. The author also reports that a percentage of immigrants with a high-school degree rose from 57.3 percent to 61.7 percent. Immigrants household income is also said to have grown from about $42,000 to $46,000 (adjusted for inflation), and the rate of poverty among this group fell from 13 to 12.1 percent. When these numbers are disaggregated, one observes the emergence of some divergent trends among some immigrant groups.

For example, while 66 percent of Indian immigrants hold a college degree, there are only 3 percent of Mexican immigrants that hold a college degree. Poverty rates range from 23.1 percent among persons from Bosnia-Herzegovina to only 2.2 percent among Filipinos. The Filipino median household is a remarkable $73,000 compared to $23,000 for Ukraine-born households. There is continued growth among Mexican immigrants and Indians, as well as high percentage growth among certain groups from sub-Saharan Africa, such as Nigerians and Ghanaians (both groups tripled their size in the 1990s).

The city and state governments are called upon to play a proactive role in promoting the drive toward comprehensive immigration reform; an idea that may have suffered greatly as a result of the recent general elections. City governance processes and policy approaches should also be geared at bridging some of the socio-economic gaps among immigrant communities as well as between immigrants and native born Americans who are residents of the city.

CONCLUSION

In this essay, this researcher discussed the characteristics of metropolitan Chicago's global city status. The analysis in this essay rested on a central proposition that proactive policies at the municipal and state levels are essential to maintaining metropolitan Chicago's global city status. The researcher concludes that determined policy and strategic actions at the levels of city and state governments are required to undergird Chicago's global city status. The researcher also concludes that these efforts will be influenced by globalization processes that affect a range of issues, including technology, urban policy, and patterns of migration to the city. It is also suggested that these trends and issues will help to define the role and fundamental character of MNCs headquartered in Chicago.

REFERENCES

Birkland, T. A. (2005). *An Introduction to the Policy Process: Theories, Concepts, and Models of Public Policy.* New York: M.E. Sharpe.

Brenner, N., & Theodore, N. (2005). Neoliberalism and the Urban Condition. *City, 9*(1), 101–107. doi:10.1080/13604810500092106

Buechler, S. (2002). Sao Paulo: Outsourcing and Downgrading of Labor in a Globalizing City. In N. Brenner & R. Keil (Eds.), *The Global Reader* (pp. 228–245). London: Routledge.

Chalana, M. (2012). Of Mills and Malls: The Future of Urban Industrial Heritage in Neo-Liberal Mumbai. *Futur Anterieur, 9*(1), 1–8.

Chattopadhyay, S. (2015). Contesting Inclusiveness: Policies Politics and Processes of Participatory Urban Governance in Indian Cities. *Progress in Development Studies, 15*(1), 22–36. doi:10.1177/1464993414546969

Drennan, P. M. (1988). Information Intensive Industries in Metropolitan Areas of the United States of America. *Environment & Planning, 21*(12), 1603–1618. doi:10.1068/a211603

Dye, T. R. (1981). *Understanding Public Policy*. New Jersey: Prentice Hall, Inc.

Fainstein, S. S. (2012). Inequality in Global Regions. *The Planning Review, 37*(144), 20–25. doi:10.1080/02513625.2001.10556764

Freitag, B. (2003). Global Cities in Informational Societies. *Diogenes, 50*(1), 71–82. doi:10.1177/039219210305000108

Friedmann, J. (1986). The World City Hypothesis. *Development and Change, 17*(1), 69–83. doi:10.1111/j.1467-7660.1986.tb00231.x

Frost, M., & Spence, N. (1993). Global City Characteristics and Central London's Employment. *Urban Studies, 30*(3), 547–558. doi:10.1080/00420989320080541

Grant, R., & Nijman, J. (2006). Globalization and the Corporate Geography of Cities in the Less-Developed World. In N. Brenner & R. Keil (Eds.), *The Global Cities Reader* (pp. 225–237). New York: Routledge.

Hayes, M. T. (2007). Policy Characteristics, Patterns of Politics, and the Minimum Wage: Toward a Typology of Redistributive Policies. *Policy Studies Journal: the Journal of the Policy Studies Organization, 35*(3), 465–480. doi:10.1111/j.1541-0072.2007.00233.x

Heysse, T. (2006). Consensus and Power in Deliberative Democracy. *Inquiry, 49*(3), 265–289. doi:10.1080/00201740600725723

Kearney, A. T. (2014). 2014 Global Cities Index and Emerging Cities Outlook. Chicago.

Kearney, A.T., & McCann, E.J. (2004). Urban Political Economy Beyond the Global City. *Urban Studies, 41*(12), 2315–23333.

Merrilees, B., Miller, D., & Herrington, C. (2013). City Branding: A Facilitating Framework for Stressed Cities. *Journal of Business Research, 66*(1), 37–44. doi:10.1016/j.jbusres.2011.07.021

Murray, M. J. (2004). *The Evolving Spatial Form of Cities in a Globalizing World Economy*. Cape Town: HSRC Publishers.

Neal, Z. (2011). Differentiating Centrality and Power in the World City Network. *Urban Studies (Edinburgh, Scotland), 48*(13), 2733–2748. doi:10.1177/0042098010388954

Nijman, J. (2008). Against the Odds: Slum Rehabilitation in Neoliberal Mumbai. *Cities (London, England), 25*(2), 73–85. doi:10.1016/j.cities.2008.01.003

Olds, K., & Yeung, H. (2011). Pathways to Global City Formation: A View from the Developmental City-State of Singapore. *Review of International Political Economy, 11*(4), 489–521.

Paral, R. (2003). Chicago's Immigrants Break Old Patterns. Retrieved from http://www.migrationpolicy.org/article/chicagos-immigrants-break-old-patterns

Phadke, A. (2014). Mumbai metropolitan region: Impact of Recent Urban Change on the Peri-Urban Areas of Mumbai. *Urban Studies, 51*(11), 2466–2483. doi:10.1177/0042098013493483

Samers, M. (2002). Immigration and the Global City Hypothesis: Towards an Alternative Research Agenda. In N. Brenner & R. Keil (Eds.), *The Global Reader* (pp. 384–391). London: Routledge. doi:10.1111/1468-2427.00386

Sassen, S. (1996). Cities and Communities in the Global Economy: Rethinking Our Concepts. *The Behavioral Scientist, 39*(5), 629–636. doi:10.1177/0002764296039005009

Sassen, S. (2006). *Cities in a world economy* (3rd ed.). Thousand Oaks: Pine Forge Press.

Sassen, S. (2010). Reading the city in a global digital age: The Limits of Topographical Representation. *Procedia: Social and Behavioral Sciences, 2*(5), 7030–7041. doi:10.1016/j.sbspro.2010.05.057

Sassen, S. (2010). The City: Its Return as a Lens for Social Theory. *City, Cultura e Scuola, 1*, 3–11.

Sassen, S. (2013). When the center no longer holds: Cities as Frontier Zones. *Cities (London, England), 34*, 67–70. doi:10.1016/j.cities.2012.05.007

Sharma, R. N. (2010). Mega Transformation of Mumbai: Deepening Enclave Urbanism. *Sociological Bulletin, 59*(1), 69–91.

Smith, M. P. (2002). The global cities discourse: A Return to the Master Narrative. In N. Brenner & R. Keil (Eds.), *The Global Reader* (pp. 238–245). London: Routledge.

Short, J. R. (2006). *Urban theory*. New York: Palgrave.

Surjan, A., & Shaw, R. (2009). Enhancing Disaster Resilience Through Local Environment Management: Case of Mumbai, India. *Disaster Prevention and Management*, *18*(4), 418–433. doi:10.1108/09653560910984474

Widmayer, P. (2000). Transforming a Global City for the Information Society: Metropolitan Chicago at the Crossroads. *Journal of Urban Technology*, *7*(2), 23–42. doi:10.1080/713684109

Yella, S. (2006). Dynamics of Environmental Problems in Mumbai. *Clean Technology Environmental Policy*, *8*(3), 182–187. doi:10.1007/s10098-005-0030-7

Zerah, M.-H. (2009). Participatory governance in Urban Management and the Shifting Geometry of Power in Mumbai. *Development and Change*, *40*(5), 853–877. doi:10.1111/j.1467-7660.2009.01586.x

Related Readings

To continue IGI Global's long-standing tradition of advancing innovation through emerging research, please find below a compiled list of recommended IGI Global book chapters and journal articles in the areas of economics, global economies, and business markets. These related readings will provide additional information and guidance to further enrich your knowledge and assist you with your own research.

Abdul-Mohsin, A. (2017). The Relationship between Entrepreneurial Competencies, Competitive Intelligence, and Innovative Performance among SMEs from an Emerging Country: Competitive Intelligence in SMEs. In I. Hosu & I. Iancu (Eds.), *Digital Entrepreneurship and Global Innovation* (pp. 37–58). Hershey, PA: IGI Global. doi:10.4018/978-1-5225-0953-0.ch003

Abubakre, M., Coombs, C. R., & Ravishankar, M. N. (2017). The Impact of Salient Cultural Practices on the Outcome of IS Implementation. *Journal of Global Information Management, 25*(1), 1–20. doi:10.4018/JGIM.2017010101

Agrawal, H. O. (2016). An Approach to Business Strategy. In U. Panwar, R. Kumar, & N. Ray (Eds.), *Handbook of Research on Promotional Strategies and Consumer Influence in the Service Sector* (pp. 154–182). Hershey, PA: IGI Global. doi:10.4018/978-1-5225-0143-5.ch009

Allegreni, F. (2017). Crowdfunding as a Marketing Tool. In W. Vassallo (Ed.), *Crowdfunding for Sustainable Entrepreneurship and Innovation* (pp. 187–203). Hershey, PA: IGI Global. doi:10.4018/978-1-5225-0568-6.ch011

Ambani, P. (2017). Crowdsourcing New Tools to Start Lean and Succeed in Entrepreneurship: Entrepreneurship in the Crowd Economy. In W. Vassallo (Ed.), *Crowdfunding for Sustainable Entrepreneurship and Innovation* (pp. 37–53). Hershey, PA: IGI Global. doi:10.4018/978-1-5225-0568-6.ch003

Amone, W. (2015). Global Market Trends. In B. Christiansen (Ed.), *Handbook of Research on Global Business Opportunities* (pp. 37–58). Hershey, PA: IGI Global. doi:10.4018/978-1-4666-6551-4.ch002

Aryanto, V. D. (2017). The Role of Local Wisdom-Based e-Eco-Innovation to Promote Firms Marketing Performance. *International Journal of Social Ecology and Sustainable Development*, 8(1), 17–31. doi:10.4018/IJSESD.2017010102

Asturias, L. R. (2016). Business Development Opportunities and Market Entry Challenges in Latin America. In M. Garita & J. Godinez (Eds.), *Business Development Opportunities and Market Entry Challenges in Latin America* (pp. 256–271). Hershey, PA: IGI Global. doi:10.4018/978-1-4666-8820-9.ch012

Ayari, A. (2016). Corporate Social Responsibility in the Bahraini Construction Companies. In M. Al-Shammari & H. Masri (Eds.), *Ethical and Social Perspectives on Global Business Interaction in Emerging Markets* (pp. 40–51). Hershey, PA: IGI Global. doi:10.4018/978-1-4666-9864-2.ch003

Baporikar, N. (2017). Business Excellence Strategies for SME Sustainability in India. In P. Ordóñez de Pablos (Ed.), *Managerial Strategies and Solutions for Business Success in Asia* (pp. 61–78). Hershey, PA: IGI Global. doi:10.4018/978-1-5225-1886-0.ch004

Baranowska-Prokop, E., & Sikora, T. (2017). Competitiveness of Polish International New Ventures from Managerial Perspective. In A. Vlachvei, O. Notta, K. Karantininis, & N. Tsounis (Eds.), *Factors Affecting Firm Competitiveness and Performance in the Modern Business World* (pp. 83–107). Hershey, PA: IGI Global. doi:10.4018/978-1-5225-0843-4.ch003

Bartens, Y., Chunpir, H. I., Schulte, F., & Voß, S. (2017). Business/IT Alignment in Two-Sided Markets: A COBIT 5 Analysis for Media Streaming Business Models. In S. De Haes & W. Van Grembergen (Eds.), *Strategic IT Governance and Alignment in Business Settings* (pp. 82–111). Hershey, PA: IGI Global. doi:10.4018/978-1-5225-0861-8.ch004

Beharry-Ramraj, A. (2016). Business Strategies Creating Value for Social Entrepreneurs. In Z. Fields (Ed.), *Incorporating Business Models and Strategies into Social Entrepreneurship* (pp. 80–96). Hershey, PA: IGI Global. doi:10.4018/978-1-4666-8748-6.ch005

Bernardino, J., & Neves, P. C. (2016). Decision-Making with Big Data Using Open Source Business Intelligence Systems. In H. Rahman (Ed.), *Human Development and Interaction in the Age of Ubiquitous Technology* (pp. 120–147). Hershey, PA: IGI Global. doi:10.4018/978-1-5225-0556-3.ch006

Bodea, C., Stelian, S., & Mogos, R. (2017). E-Learning Solution for Enhancing Entrepreneurship Competencies in the Service Sector. In I. Hosu & I. Iancu (Eds.), *Digital Entrepreneurship and Global Innovation* (pp. 225–244). Hershey, PA: IGI Global. doi:10.4018/978-1-5225-0953-0.ch011

Bojorges Moctezuma, N. P. (2017). Consumer Impetuosity in M-Commerce: Designing Scale to Measure the Shopping Behavior. In Rajagopal, & R. Behl (Eds.), Business Analytics and Cyber Security Management in Organizations (pp. 84-105). Hershey, PA: IGI Global. doi:10.4018/978-1-5225-0902-8.ch007

Bowen, G., & Bowen, D. (2017). Strategist: Role and Attributes. In V. Wang (Ed.), *Encyclopedia of Strategic Leadership and Management* (pp. 1745–1757). Hershey, PA: IGI Global. doi:10.4018/978-1-5225-1049-9.ch121

Breuer, W., Quinten, B., & Salzmann, A. J. (2015). Bank vs. Bond Finance: A Cultural View of Corporate Debt Financing. In B. Christiansen (Ed.), *Handbook of Research on Global Business Opportunities* (pp. 289–315). Hershey, PA: IGI Global. doi:10.4018/978-1-4666-6551-4.ch014

Bruno, G. (2017). A Dataflow-Oriented Modeling Approach to Business Processes. *International Journal of Human Capital and Information Technology Professionals*, 8(1), 51–65. doi:10.4018/IJHCITP.2017010104

Can, M., & Doğan, B. (2017). The Effects of Economic Structural Transformation on Employment: An Evaluation in the Context of Economic Complexity and Product Space Theory. In F. Yenilmez & E. Kılıç (Eds.), *Handbook of Research on Unemployment and Labor Market Sustainability in the Era of Globalization* (pp. 275–306). Hershey, PA: IGI Global. doi:10.4018/978-1-5225-2008-5.ch016

Carvalheira, A. M., & Moreira, A. C. (2016). Searching for Opportunities and Trust in International Markets: Entrepreneurial Perspective of a Traditional Industry SME. In L. Carvalho (Ed.), *Handbook of Research on Entrepreneurial Success and its Impact on Regional Development* (pp. 675–701). Hershey, PA: IGI Global. doi:10.4018/978-1-4666-9567-2.ch028

Carvalho, L., Camacho, N., Amorim, G., & Esperança, J. P. (2016). Transnational Acceleration of Local Startups: Portugal's Building Global Innovators (BGI) Model. In L. Carvalho (Ed.), *Handbook of Research on Entrepreneurial Success and its Impact on Regional Development* (pp. 41–71). Hershey, PA: IGI Global. doi:10.4018/978-1-4666-9567-2.ch003

Castro, O. A., Arias, C. L., Ibañez, J. E., & Bulla, F. J. (2017). Universities Fostering Business Development: The Role of Education in Entrepreneurship. In I. Hosu & I. Iancu (Eds.), *Digital Entrepreneurship and Global Innovation* (pp. 193–224). Hershey, PA: IGI Global. doi:10.4018/978-1-5225-0953-0.ch010

Chaudhuri, S. (2016). Application of Web-Based Geographical Information System (GIS) in E-Business. In U. Panwar, R. Kumar, & N. Ray (Eds.), *Handbook of Research on Promotional Strategies and Consumer Influence in the Service Sector* (pp. 389–405). Hershey, PA: IGI Global. doi:10.4018/978-1-5225-0143-5.ch023

Chauhan, R. S., & Das, R. (2017). Entrepreneurship Policy Framework: Understanding Cultural and Educational Determinants for Entrepreneurship. In G. Afolayan & A. Akinwale (Eds.), *Global Perspectives on Development Administration and Cultural Change* (pp. 95–139). Hershey, PA: IGI Global. doi:10.4018/978-1-5225-0629-4.ch005

Chen, Y. (2017). Sustainable Supply Chains and International Soft Landings: A Case of Wetland Entrepreneurship. In B. Christiansen & F. Kasarcı (Eds.), *Corporate Espionage, Geopolitics, and Diplomacy Issues in International Business* (pp. 232–247). Hershey, PA: IGI Global. doi:10.4018/978-1-5225-1031-4.ch013

Choudhury, M. A. (2017). Cybernetic Approach for the Stock Market: An Empirical Study of Bangladesh. In I. Oncioiu (Ed.), *Driving Innovation and Business Success in the Digital Economy* (pp. 193–210). Hershey, PA: IGI Global. doi:10.4018/978-1-5225-1779-5.ch013

Christansen, B., Dirikan, T., Dirikan, C., & Kasarcı, F. (2016). Turkey's Economic Sustainability in Global Hypercompetition. In N. Zakaria, A. Abdul-Talib, & N. Osman (Eds.), *Handbook of Research on Impacts of International Business and Political Affairs on the Global Economy* (pp. 173–184). Hershey, PA: IGI Global. doi:10.4018/978-1-4666-9806-2.ch009

Cinelli, S. A. (2017). The World's Oldest Profession - Now and Then: Disruption of the Commercial Banking Model. In W. Vassallo (Ed.), *Crowdfunding for Sustainable Entrepreneurship and Innovation* (pp. 78–89). Hershey, PA: IGI Global. doi:10.4018/978-1-5225-0568-6.ch005

Cvijanovic, D., & Mihailović, B. (2016). Effects of Globalization on Economies in Transition. In V. Erokhin (Ed.), *Global Perspectives on Trade Integration and Economies in Transition* (pp. 26–44). Hershey, PA: IGI Global. doi:10.4018/978-1-5225-0451-1.ch002

Daidj, N. (2015). A Dynamic Vision of Value Chains: From Value Chains to Business Models (BM). In *Developing Strategic Business Models and Competitive Advantage in the Digital Sector* (pp. 156–182). Hershey, PA: IGI Global. doi:10.4018/978-1-4666-6513-2.ch006

Daidj, N. (2015). Disruptive Technologies, Innovation, and Competition in the Digital Economy. In *Developing Strategic Business Models and Competitive Advantage in the Digital Sector* (pp. 183–211). Hershey, PA: IGI Global. doi:10.4018/978-1-4666-6513-2.ch007

Dau, L. A., Moore, E. M., Soto, M. A., & LeBlanc, C. R. (2017). How Globalization Sparked Entrepreneurship in the Developing World: The Impact of Formal Economic and Political Linkages. In B. Christiansen & F. Kasarcı (Eds.), *Corporate Espionage, Geopolitics, and Diplomacy Issues in International Business* (pp. 72–91). Hershey, PA: IGI Global. doi:10.4018/978-1-5225-1031-4.ch005

de Burgh-Woodman, H., Bressan, A., & Torrisi, A. (2017). An Evaluation of the State of the CSR Field in Australia: Perspectives from the Banking and Mining Sectors. In D. Jamali (Ed.), *Comparative Perspectives on Global Corporate Social Responsibility* (pp. 138–164). Hershey, PA: IGI Global. doi:10.4018/978-1-5225-0720-8.ch007

De Moraes, A. J., Ekanem, I., & Osabutey, E. (2017). New Perspectives on the Internationalisation of Micro-Businesses. In S. Ojo (Ed.), *Diasporas and Transnational Entrepreneurship in Global Contexts* (pp. 115–129). Hershey, PA: IGI Global. doi:10.4018/978-1-5225-1991-1.ch007

Demiray, M., Burnaz, S., & Aslanbay, Y. (2017). The Crowdfunding Market, Models, Platforms, and Projects. In W. Vassallo (Ed.), *Crowdfunding for Sustainable Entrepreneurship and Innovation* (pp. 90–126). Hershey, PA: IGI Global. doi:10.4018/978-1-5225-0568-6.ch006

Di Fatta, D., Musotto, R., D'Aleo, V., Vesperi, W., Morabito, G., & Lo Bue, S. (2017). Weak Ties and Value of a Network in the New Internet Economy. In S. Hai-Jew (Ed.), *Social Media Data Extraction and Content Analysis* (pp. 66–84). Hershey, PA: IGI Global. doi:10.4018/978-1-5225-0648-5.ch003

Diehl, M. (2016). Financial Market Infrastructures: The Backbone of Financial Systems. In M. Diehl, B. Alexandrova-Kabadjova, R. Heuver, & S. Martínez-Jaramillo (Eds.), *Analyzing the Economics of Financial Market Infrastructures* (pp. 1–19). Hershey, PA: IGI Global. doi:10.4018/978-1-4666-8745-5.ch001

Eftonova, T., Kiran, M., & Stannett, M. (2017). Long-term Macroeconomic Dynamics of Competition in the Russian Economy using Agent- based Modelling. *International Journal of System Dynamics Applications*, 6(1), 1–20. doi:10.4018/IJSDA.2017010101

Ekanem, I., & Uwajeh, N. J. (2017). Transnational Entrepreneurs and Their Global Market Entry Modes. In S. Ojo (Ed.), *Diasporas and Transnational Entrepreneurship in Global Contexts* (pp. 130–151). Hershey, PA: IGI Global. doi:10.4018/978-1-5225-1991-1.ch008

El Dessouky, N. F. (2016). Corporate Social Responsibility of Public Banking Sector for Sustainable Development: A Comparative Study between Malaysia and Egypt. In M. Al-Shammari & H. Masri (Eds.), *Ethical and Social Perspectives on Global Business Interaction in Emerging Markets* (pp. 52–73). Hershey, PA: IGI Global. doi:10.4018/978-1-4666-9864-2.ch004

Encinas-Ferrer, C. (2017). Currency Parity and Competitiveness: The Case of Greece. In A. Vlachvei, O. Notta, K. Karantininis, & N. Tsounis (Eds.), *Factors Affecting Firm Competitiveness and Performance in the Modern Business World* (pp. 282–299). Hershey, PA: IGI Global. doi:10.4018/978-1-5225-0843-4.ch010

Firdhous, M. F. (2015). Strategies for Evaluating Cloud System Providers during the Transformation of Businesses. In F. Soliman (Ed.), *Business Transformation and Sustainability through Cloud System Implementation* (pp. 58–77). Hershey, PA: IGI Global. doi:10.4018/978-1-4666-6445-6.ch005

Garo, E. (2017). Gap Between Theory and Practice in Management Education: Teaching Entrepreneurship Through Practice. In D. Latusek (Ed.), *Case Studies as a Teaching Tool in Management Education* (pp. 264–277). Hershey, PA: IGI Global. doi:10.4018/978-1-5225-0770-3.ch014

Gençer, M., & Oba, B. (2017). Taming of "Openness" in Software Innovation Systems. In I. Oncioiu (Ed.), *Driving Innovation and Business Success in the Digital Economy* (pp. 26–40). Hershey, PA: IGI Global. doi:10.4018/978-1-5225-1779-5.ch003

Gianni, M., & Gotzamani, K. (2016). Integrated Management Systems and Information Management Systems: Common Threads. In P. Papajorgji, F. Pinet, A. Guimarães, & J. Papathanasiou (Eds.), *Automated Enterprise Systems for Maximizing Business Performance* (pp. 195–214). Hershey, PA: IGI Global. doi:10.4018/978-1-4666-8841-4.ch011

Goerlach, C., Brehm, A., & Lonnen, B. (2016). FMIs – Knights in Shining Armour? In M. Diehl, B. Alexandrova-Kabadjova, R. Heuver, & S. Martínez-Jaramillo (Eds.), *Analyzing the Economics of Financial Market Infrastructures* (pp. 71–89). Hershey, PA: IGI Global. doi:10.4018/978-1-4666-8745-5.ch004

Hamidi, H. (2017). A Model for Impact of Organizational Project Benefits Management and its Impact on End User. *Journal of Organizational and End User Computing*, 29(1), 51–65. doi:10.4018/JOEUC.2017010104

Hartlieb, S., & Silvius, G. (2017). Handling Uncertainty in Project Management and Business Development: Similarities and Differences. In Y. Raydugin (Ed.), *Handbook of Research on Leveraging Risk and Uncertainties for Effective Project Management* (pp. 337–362). Hershey, PA: IGI Global. doi:10.4018/978-1-5225-1790-0.ch016

Haynes, J. D., Arockiasamy, S., Al Rashdi, M., & Al Rashdi, S. (2016). Business and E Business Strategies for Coopetition and Thematic Management as a Sustained Basis for Ethics and Social Responsibility in Emerging Markets. In M. Al-Shammari & H. Masri (Eds.), *Ethical and Social Perspectives on Global Business Interaction in Emerging Markets* (pp. 25–39). Hershey, PA: IGI Global. doi:10.4018/978-1-4666-9864-2.ch002

Heuver, R., & Heijmans, R. (2016). Using FMI Transaction Data in Simulations: Less Is More? In M. Diehl, B. Alexandrova-Kabadjova, R. Heuver, & S. Martínez-Jaramillo (Eds.), *Analyzing the Economics of Financial Market Infrastructures* (pp. 102–123). Hershey, PA: IGI Global. doi:10.4018/978-1-4666-8745-5.ch006

Homata, A., Mihiotis, A., & Tzortzaki, A. M. (2017). Franchise Management and the Greek Franchise Industry. In A. Vlachvei, O. Notta, K. Karantininis, & N. Tsounis (Eds.), *Factors Affecting Firm Competitiveness and Performance in the Modern Business World* (pp. 251–281). Hershey, PA: IGI Global. doi:10.4018/978-1-5225-0843-4.ch009

Huang, L. K. (2017). A Cultural Model of Online Banking Adoption: Long-Term Orientation Perspective. *Journal of Organizational and End User Computing, 29*(1), 1–22. doi:10.4018/JOEUC.2017010101

Hunter, M. G. (2015). Adoption. In *Strategic Utilization of Information Systems in Small Business* (pp. 136–169). Hershey, PA: IGI Global. doi:10.4018/978-1-4666-8708-0.ch005

Hunter, M. G. (2015). E-Business. In *Strategic Utilization of Information Systems in Small Business* (pp. 241–256). Hershey, PA: IGI Global. doi:10.4018/978-1-4666-8708-0.ch011

Hunter, M. G. (2015). Entrepreneurs' Contributions to Small Business: A Comparison of Success and Failure. In B. Christiansen (Ed.), *Handbook of Research on Global Business Opportunities* (pp. 168–198). Hershey, PA: IGI Global. doi:10.4018/978-1-4666-6551-4.ch008

Hunter, M. G. (2015). Information Systems. In *Strategic Utilization of Information Systems in Small Business* (pp. 78–108). Hershey, PA: IGI Global. doi:10.4018/978-1-4666-8708-0.ch003

Hunter, M. G. (2015). Management Processes. In *Strategic Utilization of Information Systems in Small Business* (pp. 211–225). Hershey, PA: IGI Global. doi:10.4018/978-1-4666-8708-0.ch009

Hunter, M. G. (2015). Theories for Investigations. In *Strategic Utilization of Information Systems in Small Business* (pp. 109–135). Hershey, PA: IGI Global. doi:10.4018/978-1-4666-8708-0.ch004

Ianole, R. (2014). An Empirical Exploration of Mental Representations in the Individual Saving Decision Process. *International Journal of Applied Behavioral Economics*, *3*(3), 48–63. doi:10.4018/ijabe.2014070104

Igbinakhase, I. (2017). Responsible and Sustainable Management Practices in Developing and Developed Business Environments. In Z. Fields (Ed.), *Collective Creativity for Responsible and Sustainable Business Practice* (pp. 180–207). Hershey, PA: IGI Global. doi:10.4018/978-1-5225-1823-5.ch010

Iwaloye, O. O., & Shi, G. J. (2016). Market Receptiveness and Product Positioning Model of Chinese Firms in Emerging Markets. In A. Gbadamosi (Ed.), *Handbook of Research on Consumerism and Buying Behavior in Developing Nations* (pp. 99–119). Hershey, PA: IGI Global. doi:10.4018/978-1-5225-0282-1.ch005

Iwata, J. J., & Hoskins, R. G. (2017). Managing Indigenous Knowledge in Tanzania: A Business Perspective. In P. Jain & N. Mnjama (Eds.), *Managing Knowledge Resources and Records in Modern Organizations* (pp. 198–214). Hershey, PA: IGI Global. doi:10.4018/978-1-5225-1965-2.ch012

Jain, P. (2017). A Crowd-Funder Value (CFV) Framework for Crowd-Investment: A Roadmap for Entrepreneurial Success in the Contemporary Society. In W. Vassallo (Ed.), *Crowdfunding for Sustainable Entrepreneurship and Innovation* (pp. 288–309). Hershey, PA: IGI Global. doi:10.4018/978-1-5225-0568-6.ch016

Jasmine, K. S., & Sudha, M. (2015). Business Transformation though Cloud Computing in Sustainable Business. In F. Soliman (Ed.), *Business Transformation and Sustainability through Cloud System Implementation* (pp. 44–57). Hershey, PA: IGI Global. doi:10.4018/978-1-4666-6445-6.ch004

Jihene, M. (2016). Women's Empowerment and Socio-Economic Development in MENA Region: Adaptation to Trade Policies and Access to Market for Promoting Entrepreneurship. In S. Sen, A. Bhattacharya, & R. Sen (Eds.), *International Perspectives on Socio-Economic Development in the Era of Globalization* (pp. 113–128). Hershey, PA: IGI Global. doi:10.4018/978-1-4666-9908-3.ch007

Kamasak, R., & Yavuz, M. (2016). Economic Development, Market Characteristics and Current Business Conditions in Turkey: A Guide for Successful Business Operations. In B. Christiansen & M. Erdoğdu (Eds.), *Comparative Economics and Regional Development in Turkey* (pp. 336–354). Hershey, PA: IGI Global. doi:10.4018/978-1-4666-8729-5.ch016

Kaplan, Z. (2017). The EU's Internal Market and the Free Movement of Labor: Economic Effects and Challenges. In F. Yenilmez & E. Kılıç (Eds.), *Handbook of Research on Unemployment and Labor Market Sustainability in the Era of Globalization* (pp. 61–75). Hershey, PA: IGI Global. doi:10.4018/978-1-5225-2008-5.ch005

Kasemsap, K. (2016). Exploring the Roles of Entrepreneurship and Internationalization in Global Business. In L. Carvalho (Ed.), *Handbook of Research on Entrepreneurial Success and its Impact on Regional Development* (pp. 481–512). Hershey, PA: IGI Global. doi:10.4018/978-1-4666-9567-2.ch021

Kasemsap, K. (2017). Mastering Business Process Management and Business Intelligence in Global Business. In M. Tavana, K. Szabat, & K. Puranam (Eds.), *Organizational Productivity and Performance Measurements Using Predictive Modeling and Analytics* (pp. 192–212). Hershey, PA: IGI Global. doi:10.4018/978-1-5225-0654-6.ch010

Kasemsap, K. (2017). The Importance of Entrepreneurship in Global Business. In B. Christiansen & F. Kasarcı (Eds.), *Corporate Espionage, Geopolitics, and Diplomacy Issues in International Business* (pp. 92–115). Hershey, PA: IGI Global. doi:10.4018/978-1-5225-1031-4.ch006

Kaushal, L. A. (2016). Multinational Corporations: A Boon or Bane for a Developing Economy – A Study in Indian Context. In N. Zakaria, A. Abdul-Talib, & N. Osman (Eds.), *Handbook of Research on Impacts of International Business and Political Affairs on the Global Economy* (pp. 154–172). Hershey, PA: IGI Global. doi:10.4018/978-1-4666-9806-2.ch008

Kavoura, A., & Koziol, L. (2017). Polish Firms' Innovation Capability for Competitiveness via Information Technologies and Social Media Implementation. In A. Vlachvei, O. Notta, K. Karantininis, & N. Tsounis (Eds.), *Factors Affecting Firm Competitiveness and Performance in the Modern Business World* (pp. 191–222). Hershey, PA: IGI Global. doi:10.4018/978-1-5225-0843-4.ch007

Khalique, M., Shaari, J. A., & Isa, A. H. (2015). A Descriptive Study of Intellectual Capital in SMEs Operating in Electrical and Electronics Manufacturing Sector in Malaysia. In P. Ordoñez de Pablos, L. Turró, R. Tennyson, & J. Zhao (Eds.), *Knowledge Management for Competitive Advantage During Economic Crisis* (pp. 1–15). Hershey, PA: IGI Global. doi:10.4018/978-1-4666-6457-9.ch001

Khan, I. U., Hameed, Z., & Khan, S. U. (2017). Understanding Online Banking Adoption in a Developing Country: UTAUT2 with Cultural Moderators. *Journal of Global Information Management*, 25(1), 43–65. doi:10.4018/JGIM.2017010103

Kiregian, E. (2017). The Transformation of Russian Business Education and Its Outcomes: How Russia Moved Away from Marxism toward a Market Economy through Revitalized Business Education. In F. Topor (Ed.), *Handbook of Research on Individualism and Identity in the Globalized Digital Age* (pp. 457–477). Hershey, PA: IGI Global. doi:10.4018/978-1-5225-0522-8.ch020

Kofahi, I., & Alryalat, H. (2017). Enterprise Resource Planning (ERP) Implementation Approaches and the Performance of Procure-to-Pay Business Processes: (Field Study in Companies that Implement Oracle ERP in Jordan). *International Journal of Information Technology Project Management*, 8(1), 55–71. doi:10.4018/IJITPM.2017010104

Kożuch, B., & Jabłoński, A. (2017). Adopting the Concept of Business Models in Public Management. In M. Lewandowski & B. Kożuch (Eds.), *Public Sector Entrepreneurship and the Integration of Innovative Business Models* (pp. 10–46). Hershey, PA: IGI Global. doi:10.4018/978-1-5225-2215-7.ch002

Kumar, M. (2017). A Panel Data Analysis for Exploring the New Determinants of Growth in Small and Medium Sized Enterprises in India. *International Journal of Asian Business and Information Management*, 8(1), 1–23. doi:10.4018/IJABIM.2017010101

Kumar, M. (2017). Profitability of Indian Firms in Foreign Direct Investment. *International Journal of Asian Business and Information Management*, 8(1), 51–67. doi:10.4018/IJABIM.2017010104

Laine, T. A., & Korpinen, K. (2016). Exploiting Parallelization to Increase the Performance of Payment Systems Simulations. In M. Diehl, B. Alexandrova-Kabadjova, R. Heuver, & S. Martínez-Jaramillo (Eds.), *Analyzing the Economics of Financial Market Infrastructures* (pp. 91–101). Hershey, PA: IGI Global. doi:10.4018/978-1-4666-8745-5.ch005

Lavassani, K. M., & Movahedi, B. (2017). Applications Driven Information Systems: Beyond Networks toward Business Ecosystems. In I. Oncioiu (Ed.), *Driving Innovation and Business Success in the Digital Economy* (pp. 159–171). Hershey, PA: IGI Global. doi:10.4018/978-1-5225-1779-5.ch011

Le, N., Li, X., & Yukhanaev, A. (2015). Locational Determinants of Foreign Direct Investment in the Vietnamese Economy. In B. Christiansen (Ed.), *Handbook of Research on Global Business Opportunities* (pp. 1–36). Hershey, PA: IGI Global. doi:10.4018/978-1-4666-6551-4.ch001

Lederer, M., Kurz, M., & Lazarov, P. (2017). Usage and Suitability of Methods for Strategic Business Process Initiatives: A Multi Case Study Research. *International Journal of Productivity Management and Assessment Technologies, 5*(1), 40–51. doi:10.4018/IJPMAT.2017010103

Lee, I. (2017). A Social Enterprise Business Model and a Case Study of Pacific Community Ventures (PCV). In V. Potocan, M. Üngan, & Z. Nedelko (Eds.), *Handbook of Research on Managerial Solutions in Non-Profit Organizations* (pp. 182–204). Hershey, PA: IGI Global. doi:10.4018/978-1-5225-0731-4.ch009

León, C., Pérez, J., & Renneboog, L. (2016). A Multi-Layer Network of the Colombian Sovereign Securities Market. In M. Diehl, B. Alexandrova-Kabadjova, R. Heuver, & S. Martínez-Jaramillo (Eds.), *Analyzing the Economics of Financial Market Infrastructures* (pp. 124–149). Hershey, PA: IGI Global. doi:10.4018/978-1-4666-8745-5.ch007

Lewandowski, M. (2017). Public Organizations and Business Model Innovation: The Role of Public Service Design. In M. Lewandowski & B. Kożuch (Eds.), *Public Sector Entrepreneurship and the Integration of Innovative Business Models* (pp. 47–72). Hershey, PA: IGI Global. doi:10.4018/978-1-5225-2215-7.ch003

Liu, H., Ke, W., Wei, K. K., & Lu, Y. (2016). The Effects of Social Capital on Firm Substantive and Symbolic Performance: In the Context of E-Business. *Journal of Global Information Management*, 24(1), 61–85. doi:10.4018/JGIM.2016010104

Magala, S. J. (2017). Between Davos and Porto Alegre: Democratic Entrepreneurship as Crowdsourcing for Ideas. In M. Lewandowski & B. Kożuch (Eds.), *Public Sector Entrepreneurship and the Integration of Innovative Business Models* (pp. 1–9). Hershey, PA: IGI Global. doi:10.4018/978-1-5225-2215-7.ch001

Mandal, R., & Nath, H. K. (2017). Services Trade in Emerging Market Economies. In Rajagopal, & R. Behl (Eds.), Business Analytics and Cyber Security Management in Organizations (pp. 64-83). Hershey, PA: IGI Global. doi:10.4018/978-1-5225-0902-8.ch006

Mangalaraj, G., & Amaravadi, C. S. (2016). The B2B Market Place: A Review and a Typology. In I. Lee (Ed.), *Encyclopedia of E-Commerce Development, Implementation, and Management* (pp. 905–915). Hershey, PA: IGI Global. doi:10.4018/978-1-4666-9787-4.ch064

Martinez-Jaramillo, S., Molina-Borboa, J. L., & Bravo-Benitez, B. (2016). The role of Financial Market Infrastructures in Financial Stability: An Overview. In M. Diehl, B. Alexandrova-Kabadjova, R. Heuver, & S. Martínez-Jaramillo (Eds.), *Analyzing the Economics of Financial Market Infrastructures* (pp. 20–40). Hershey, PA: IGI Global. doi:10.4018/978-1-4666-8745-5.ch002

Massarenti, M. (2016). Undressing the Global Derivatives Market: Trade Repositories: Past, Present and Future. In M. Diehl, B. Alexandrova-Kabadjova, R. Heuver, & S. Martínez-Jaramillo (Eds.), *Analyzing the Economics of Financial Market Infrastructures* (pp. 359–368). Hershey, PA: IGI Global. doi:10.4018/978-1-4666-8745-5.ch018

McAvoy, D. (2017). Institutional Entrepreneurship in Defence Acquisition: What Don't We Understand? In K. Burgess & P. Antill (Eds.), *Emerging Strategies in Defense Acquisitions and Military Procurement* (pp. 222–241). Hershey, PA: IGI Global. doi:10.4018/978-1-5225-0599-0.ch013

Milne, A. (2016). Central Securities Depositories and Securities Clearing and Settlement: Business Practice and Public Policy Concerns. In M. Diehl, B. Alexandrova-Kabadjova, R. Heuver, & S. Martínez-Jaramillo (Eds.), *Analyzing the Economics of Financial Market Infrastructures* (pp. 334–358). Hershey, PA: IGI Global. doi:10.4018/978-1-4666-8745-5.ch017

Mohanty, S. K. (2017). Globalization, Innovation, and Marketing Philosophy: A Critical Assessment of Role of Technology in Defining New Dimensions. In Rajagopal, & R. Behl (Eds.), Business Analytics and Cyber Security Management in Organizations (pp. 48-63). Hershey, PA: IGI Global. doi:10.4018/978-1-5225-0902-8.ch005

Moreira, A. C., & Alves, C. B. (2016). Commitment-Trust Dynamics in the Internationalization Process: A Case Study of Market Entry in the Brazilian Market. In M. Garita & J. Godinez (Eds.), *Business Development Opportunities and Market Entry Challenges in Latin America* (pp. 224–255). Hershey, PA: IGI Global. doi:10.4018/978-1-4666-8820-9.ch011

Munkata, A. S., Anin, E. K., Essuman, D., & Ataburo, H. (2017). Pursuing Supply Chain Integration: Roles of Resources, Competences, Experience, and Industry-type. *International Journal of Business Analytics*, *4*(1), 87–103. doi:10.4018/IJBAN.2017010105

Nekaj, E. L. (2017). The Crowd Economy: From the Crowd to Businesses to Public Administrations and Multinational Companies. In W. Vassallo (Ed.), *Crowdfunding for Sustainable Entrepreneurship and Innovation* (pp. 1–19). Hershey, PA: IGI Global. doi:10.4018/978-1-5225-0568-6.ch001

Nunez, S., & Castaño, R. (2017). Building Brands in Emerging Economies: A Consumer-Oriented Approach. In Rajagopal, & R. Behl (Eds.), Business Analytics and Cyber Security Management in Organizations (pp. 183-194). Hershey, PA: IGI Global. doi:10.4018/978-1-5225-0902-8.ch013

Nunez-Zabaleta, A., Olabarri, E., & Monge-Benito, S. (2017). Getting New Business Contacts in Foreign Markets through Social Networking Sites: Perspectives from Professionals of Basque Region in SPAIN. In V. Benson, R. Tuninga, & G. Saridakis (Eds.), *Analyzing the Strategic Role of Social Networking in Firm Growth and Productivity* (pp. 334–351). Hershey, PA: IGI Global. doi:10.4018/978-1-5225-0559-4.ch018

Ogrean, C., & Herciu, M. (2016). CSR Strategies in Emerging Markets: Socially Responsible Decision Making Processes and Business Practices for Sustainability. In M. Al-Shammari & H. Masri (Eds.), *Ethical and Social Perspectives on Global Business Interaction in Emerging Markets* (pp. 1–24). Hershey, PA: IGI Global. doi:10.4018/978-1-4666-9864-2.ch001

Oju, O. (2017). Impact of Innovation on the Entrepreneurial Success in Selected Business Enterprises in South-West Nigeria. In I. Oncioiu (Ed.), *Driving Innovation and Business Success in the Digital Economy* (pp. 16–25). Hershey, PA: IGI Global. doi:10.4018/978-1-5225-1779-5.ch002

Okoya, J. (2017). Interfacing with Diaspora/Ethnic Entrepreneurship: A Case of Getting the Right Balance in the HRM Ethnic Marketing Nexus. In S. Ojo (Ed.), *Diasporas and Transnational Entrepreneurship in Global Contexts* (pp. 173–187). Hershey, PA: IGI Global. doi:10.4018/978-1-5225-1991-1.ch010

Pandit, S., Milman, I., Oberhofer, M., & Zhou, Y. (2017). Principled Reference Data Management for Big Data and Business Intelligence. *International Journal of Organizational and Collective Intelligence*, 7(1), 47–66. doi:10.4018/IJOCI.2017010104

Paudel, N. P. (2016). Financial Market in Nepal: Challenges of the Financial Sector Development in Nepal. In A. Kashyap & A. Tomar (Eds.), *Financial Market Regulations and Legal Challenges in South Asia* (pp. 146–194). Hershey, PA: IGI Global. doi:10.4018/978-1-5225-0004-9.ch009

Pawliczek, A., & Rössler, M. (2017). Knowledge of Management Tools and Systems in SMEs: Knowledge Transfer in Management. In A. Bencsik (Ed.), *Knowledge Management Initiatives and Strategies in Small and Medium Enterprises* (pp. 180–203). Hershey, PA: IGI Global. doi:10.4018/978-1-5225-1642-2.ch009

Prokop, J. (2017). Firm Performance and Research and Development. In A. Vlachvei, O. Notta, K. Karantininis, & N. Tsounis (Eds.), *Factors Affecting Firm Competitiveness and Performance in the Modern Business World* (pp. 108–128). Hershey, PA: IGI Global. doi:10.4018/978-1-5225-0843-4.ch004

Qi, A., & Zheng, L. (2016). Project Risk Management: A Chinese Perspective. In C. Bodea, A. Purnus, M. Huemann, & M. Hajdu (Eds.), *Managing Project Risks for Competitive Advantage in Changing Business Environments* (pp. 45–69). Hershey, PA: IGI Global. doi:10.4018/978-1-5225-0335-4.ch003

Rajagopal. (2017). Interplay of Technology and Customer Value Dynamics in Banking Industry: Analytical Construct for Measuring Growth and Performance. In Rajagopal, & R. Behl (Eds.), *Business Analytics and Cyber Security Management in Organizations* (pp. 147-161). Hershey, PA: IGI Global. doi:10.4018/978-1-5225-0902-8.ch011

Rajagopal. (2017). Competing on Performance on the Global Marketplace: Applying Business Analytics as a Robust Decision Tool. In Rajagopal, & R. Behl (Eds.), *Business Analytics and Cyber Security Management in Organizations* (pp. 1-13). Hershey, PA: IGI Global. doi:10.4018/978-1-5225-0902-8.ch001

Rajagopal,. (2017). Role of Consumer Knowledge in Developing Purchase Intentions and Driving Services Efficiency across Marketing Channels in Mexico. In Rajagopal, & R. Behl (Eds.), *Business Analytics and Cyber Security Management in Organizations* (pp. 204-226). Hershey, PA: IGI Global. doi:10.4018/978-1-5225-0902-8.ch015

Rao, N. R. (2017). Social Media: An Enabler in Developing Business Models for Enterprises. In N. Rao (Ed.), *Social Media Listening and Monitoring for Business Applications* (pp. 165–173). Hershey, PA: IGI Global. doi:10.4018/978-1-5225-0846-5.ch009

Raue, S., & Klein, L. (2016). Systemic Risk Management: A Practice Approach to the Systemic Management of Project Risk. In C. Bodea, A. Purnus, M. Huemann, & M. Hajdu (Eds.), *Managing Project Risks for Competitive Advantage in Changing Business Environments* (pp. 70–85). Hershey, PA: IGI Global. doi:10.4018/978-1-5225-0335-4.ch004

Reyes-Mercado, P. (2017). A Readiness Index for Marketing Analytics: A Resource-Based View Conceptualization for the Implementation Stage. In Rajagopal, & R. Behl (Eds.), Business Analytics and Cyber Security Management in Organizations (pp. 38-46). Hershey, PA: IGI Global. doi:10.4018/978-1-5225-0902-8.ch004

Rosenzweig, E. D., & Bendoly, E. (2017). An Investigation of Competitor Networks in Manufacturing Strategy and Implications for Performance. In A. Vlachvei, O. Notta, K. Karantininis, & N. Tsounis (Eds.), *Factors Affecting Firm Competitiveness and Performance in the Modern Business World* (pp. 43–82). Hershey, PA: IGI Global. doi:10.4018/978-1-5225-0843-4.ch002

Rossetti di Valdalbero, D., & Birnbaum, B. (2017). Towards a New Economy: Co-Creation and Open Innovation in a Trustworthy Europe. In W. Vassallo (Ed.), *Crowdfunding for Sustainable Entrepreneurship and Innovation* (pp. 20–36). Hershey, PA: IGI Global. doi:10.4018/978-1-5225-0568-6.ch002

Ruizalba, J., & Soares, A. (2016). Internal Market Orientation and Strategy Implementation. In A. Casademunt (Ed.), *Strategic Labor Relations Management in Modern Organizations* (pp. 183–194). Hershey, PA: IGI Global. doi:10.4018/978-1-5225-0356-9.ch011

Rusko, R. (2017). Strategic Turning Points in ICT Business: The Business Development, Transformation, and Evolution in the Case of Nokia. In I. Oncioiu (Ed.), *Driving Innovation and Business Success in the Digital Economy* (pp. 1–15). Hershey, PA: IGI Global. doi:10.4018/978-1-5225-1779-5.ch001

Rusko, R., Hietanen, L., Kohtakangas, K., Kemppainen-Koivisto, R., Siltavirta, K., & Järvi, T. (2017). Educational and Business Co-Operatives: The Channels for Collective Creativity and Entrepreneurial Teams. In Z. Fields (Ed.), *Collective Creativity for Responsible and Sustainable Business Practice* (pp. 242–259). Hershey, PA: IGI Global. doi:10.4018/978-1-5225-1823-5.ch013

Saini, D. (2017). Relevance of Teaching Values and Ethics in Management Education. In N. Baporikar (Ed.), *Management Education for Global Leadership* (pp. 90–111). Hershey, PA: IGI Global. doi:10.4018/978-1-5225-1013-0.ch005

Saiz-Alvarez, J. M., Muñiz-Ávila, E., & Huezo-Ponce, D. L. (2017). Informational Competencies Entrepreneurship and Integral Values in Higher Education. In N. Baporikar (Ed.), *Innovation and Shifting Perspectives in Management Education* (pp. 79–100). Hershey, PA: IGI Global. doi:10.4018/978-1-5225-1019-2.ch004

Shaikh, F. (2017). The Benefits of New Online (Digital) Technologies on Business: Understanding the Impact of Digital on Different Aspects of the Business. In I. Hosu & I. Iancu (Eds.), *Digital Entrepreneurship and Global Innovation* (pp. 1–17). Hershey, PA: IGI Global. doi:10.4018/978-1-5225-0953-0.ch001

Silvius, G. (2016). Integrating Sustainability into Project Risk Management. In C. Bodea, A. Purnus, M. Huemann, & M. Hajdu (Eds.), *Managing Project Risks for Competitive Advantage in Changing Business Environments* (pp. 23–44). Hershey, PA: IGI Global. doi:10.4018/978-1-5225-0335-4.ch002

Soares, E. R., & Zaidan, F. H. (2017). Composition of the Financial Logistic Costs of the IT Organizations Linked to the Financial Market: Financial Indicators of the Software Development Project. In G. Jamil, A. Soares, & C. Pessoa (Eds.), *Handbook of Research on Information Management for Effective Logistics and Supply Chains* (pp. 255–272). Hershey, PA: IGI Global. doi:10.4018/978-1-5225-0973-8.ch014

Soliman, F. (2015). Could Cultural Sustainability Improve Organisational Sustainability in Cloud Environments? In F. Soliman (Ed.), *Business Transformation and Sustainability through Cloud System Implementation* (pp. 1–15). Hershey, PA: IGI Global. doi:10.4018/978-1-4666-6445-6.ch001

Soliman, F. (2015). Sustainable Business Transformation in Supply Chains. In F. Soliman (Ed.), *Business Transformation and Sustainability through Cloud System Implementation* (pp. 16–31). Hershey, PA: IGI Global. doi:10.4018/978-1-4666-6445-6.ch002

Solomon, T., & Peter, R. (2017). The Emergence of Social Media as a Contemporary Marketing Practice. In V. Benson, R. Tuninga, & G. Saridakis (Eds.), *Analyzing the Strategic Role of Social Networking in Firm Growth and Productivity* (pp. 314–333). Hershey, PA: IGI Global. doi:10.4018/978-1-5225-0559-4.ch017

Sorooshian, S. (2017). Structural Equation Modeling Algorithm and Its Application in Business Analytics. In M. Tavana, K. Szabat, & K. Puranam (Eds.), *Organizational Productivity and Performance Measurements Using Predictive Modeling and Analytics* (pp. 17–39). Hershey, PA: IGI Global. doi:10.4018/978-1-5225-0654-6.ch002

Sousa, J. C., & Gaspar, J. (2016). Start-Up: A New Conceptual Approach of Innovation Process. In A. Goel & P. Singhal (Eds.), *Product Innovation through Knowledge Management and Social Media Strategies* (pp. 291–316). Hershey, PA: IGI Global. doi:10.4018/978-1-4666-9607-5.ch013

Stancu, S., Bodea, C., Naghi, L. E., Popescu, O. M., & Neamtu, A. (2017). Use of New Innovative Technologies in Business by All Age Groups. In I. Hosu & I. Iancu (Eds.), *Digital Entrepreneurship and Global Innovation* (pp. 79–103). Hershey, PA: IGI Global. doi:10.4018/978-1-5225-0953-0.ch005

Staszewska, B. M. (2017). Local Public Enterprise Business Model as Multiple Value Creation System. In M. Lewandowski & B. Kożuch (Eds.), *Public Sector Entrepreneurship and the Integration of Innovative Business Models* (pp. 188–213). Hershey, PA: IGI Global. doi:10.4018/978-1-5225-2215-7.ch008

Sula, O., & Elenurm, T. (2017). Strategic Role of Social Networking and Personal Knowledge Management Competencies for Future Entrepreneurs. In V. Benson, R. Tuninga, & G. Saridakis (Eds.), *Analyzing the Strategic Role of Social Networking in Firm Growth and Productivity* (pp. 248–266). Hershey, PA: IGI Global. doi:10.4018/978-1-5225-0559-4.ch014

Taminiau, J., Nyangon, J., Lewis, A. S., & Byrne, J. (2017). Sustainable Business Model Innovation: Using Polycentric and Creative Climate Change Governance. In Z. Fields (Ed.), *Collective Creativity for Responsible and Sustainable Business Practice* (pp. 140–159). Hershey, PA: IGI Global. doi:10.4018/978-1-5225-1823-5.ch008

Teixeira, N., Rafael, B., & Pardal, P. (2016). Internationalization and Financial Performance: A success case in Portugal. In L. Carvalho (Ed.), *Handbook of Research on Entrepreneurial Success and its Impact on Regional Development* (pp. 88–121). Hershey, PA: IGI Global. doi:10.4018/978-1-4666-9567-2.ch005

Triandini, E., Djunaidy, A., & Siahaan, D. (2017). A Maturity Model for E-Commerce Adoption By Small And Medium Enterprises In Indonesia. *Journal of Electronic Commerce in Organizations*, *15*(1), 44–58. doi:10.4018/JECO.2017010103

Tsironis, L. K. (2016). Business Process Improvement through Data Mining Techniques: An Experimental Approach. In P. Papajorgji, F. Pinet, A. Guimarães, & J. Papathanasiou (Eds.), *Automated Enterprise Systems for Maximizing Business Performance* (pp. 150–169). Hershey, PA: IGI Global. doi:10.4018/978-1-4666-8841-4.ch009

Unterman, A. (2016). Regulating Global FMIs: Achieving Stability and Efficiency across Borders. In M. Diehl, B. Alexandrova-Kabadjova, R. Heuver, & S. Martínez-Jaramillo (Eds.), *Analyzing the Economics of Financial Market Infrastructures* (pp. 41–70). Hershey, PA: IGI Global. doi:10.4018/978-1-4666-8745-5.ch003

Van der Westhuizen, T. (2017). A Systemic Approach towards Responsible and Sustainable Economic Development: Entrepreneurship, Systems Theory, and Socio-Economic Momentum. In Z. Fields (Ed.), *Collective Creativity for Responsible and Sustainable Business Practice* (pp. 208–227). Hershey, PA: IGI Global. doi:10.4018/978-1-5225-1823-5.ch011

Vargas-Hernández, J. G., Ioannis, A. I., & González-Armenta, L. (2017). Joint Venture Efficiency through Skills Complementarity or by Reducing Transaction Costs?: A Case Study of an Apparel Company in an Emerging Market. In A. Vlachvei, O. Notta, K. Karantininis, & N. Tsounis (Eds.), *Factors Affecting Firm Competitiveness and Performance in the Modern Business World* (pp. 162–190). Hershey, PA: IGI Global. doi:10.4018/978-1-5225-0843-4.ch006

Vasudeva, S., & Singh, G. (2017). Impact of E-Core Service Quality Dimensions on Perceived Value of M-Banking in Case of Three Socio-Economic Variables. *International Journal of Technology and Human Interaction*, *13*(1), 1–20. doi:10.4018/IJTHI.2017010101

Vecchi, A., & Brennan, L. (2015). Leveraging Business Model Innovation in the International Space Industry. In B. Christiansen (Ed.), *Handbook of Research on Global Business Opportunities* (pp. 131–149). Hershey, PA: IGI Global. doi:10.4018/978-1-4666-6551-4.ch006

Vlachvei, A., & Notta, O. (2017). Firm Competitiveness: Theories, Evidence, and Measurement. In A. Vlachvei, O. Notta, K. Karantininis, & N. Tsounis (Eds.), *Factors Affecting Firm Competitiveness and Performance in the Modern Business World* (pp. 1–42). Hershey, PA: IGI Global. doi:10.4018/978-1-5225-0843-4.ch001

Wang, F., Raisinghani, M. S., Mora, M., & Wang, X. (2016). Strategic E-Business Management through a Balanced Scored Card Approach. In I. Lee (Ed.), *Encyclopedia of E-Commerce Development, Implementation, and Management* (pp. 361–386). Hershey, PA: IGI Global. doi:10.4018/978-1-4666-9787-4.ch027

Wronka-Pośpiech, M. (2017). Applying Business Solutions to Social Problems: Social Co-Operative and Its Business Model – Evidence from Poland. In M. Lewandowski & B. Kożuch (Eds.), *Public Sector Entrepreneurship and the Integration of Innovative Business Models* (pp. 139–164). Hershey, PA: IGI Global. doi:10.4018/978-1-5225-2215-7.ch006

Yama, H. (2016). A Perspective of Cross-Cultural Psychological Studies for Global Business. In N. Zakaria, A. Abdul-Talib, & N. Osman (Eds.), *Handbook of Research on Impacts of International Business and Political Affairs on the Global Economy* (pp. 185–206). Hershey, PA: IGI Global. doi:10.4018/978-1-4666-9806-2.ch010

Yang, J. G. (2016). Potentials and Perils of E-Business in China. In I. Lee (Ed.), *Encyclopedia of E-Commerce Development, Implementation, and Management* (pp. 1250–1262). Hershey, PA: IGI Global. doi:10.4018/978-1-4666-9787-4.ch090

Yaokumah, W., Kumah, P., & Okai, E. S. (2017). Demographic Influences on E-Payment Services. *International Journal of E-Business Research, 13*(1), 44–65. doi:10.4018/IJEBR.2017010103

Zhang, L. Z. (2015). Investment Strategies for Implementing Cloud Systems in Supply Chains. In F. Soliman (Ed.), *Business Transformation and Sustainability through Cloud System Implementation* (pp. 32–43). Hershey, PA: IGI Global. doi:10.4018/978-1-4666-6445-6.ch003

Zuber, C., & Pfohl, H. (2015). Cultural Management for Multinational Enterprises. In B. Christiansen (Ed.), *Handbook of Research on Global Business Opportunities* (pp. 71–102). Hershey, PA: IGI Global. doi:10.4018/978-1-4666-6551-4.ch004

About the Author

Tarnue Johnson obtained an MA in Political Economy from Middlesex University in London, UK (1992-94). Dr. Johnson completed a Postgraduate Certificate in Adult Education at the Institute of Education, University College London (1995-96). He spent a year doing postgraduate studies in Educational Research, Policy and Planning at the University of Manchester in Manchester, UK (1997-98). Dr. Johnson completed his Doctorate in Business Administration (DBA) at Argosy University with concentration in management (2007-11). He also completed Postdoctoral Studies in Public Policy at Northwestern University (2015). Dr. Johnson has authored and co-authored eleven books, including the current publication with leading American and African scholars and intellectuals. He has also written and published several peer-reviewed articles in reputable journals. Dr. Johnson has served as Senior Lecturer in business and economics at Kendall College in Chicago, Doctoral Advisor at Argosy University and Associate Vice President for Academic Support Services at Tubman University in Liberia.

Index

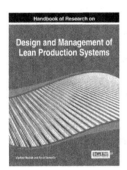
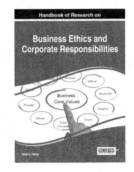

Stay Current on the Latest Emerging Research Developments

Become an IGI Global Reviewer for Authored Book Projects

Premier Reference Source

Solutions for High-Touch Communications in a High-Tech World

Premier Reference Source

Advanced Research on Biologically Inspired Cognitive Architectures

Premier Reference Source

Workforce Development Theory and Practice in the Mental Health Sector

Premier Reference Source

Resource Management and Efficiency in Cloud Computing Environments

The overall success of an authored book project is dependent on quality and timely reviews.

In this competitive age of scholarly publishing, constructive and timely feedback significantly decreases the turnaround time of manuscripts from submission to acceptance, allowing the publication and discovery of progressive research at a much more expeditious rate. Several IGI Global authored book projects are currently seeking highly qualified experts in the field to fill vacancies on their respective editorial review boards:

Applications may be sent to:
development@igi-global.com

Applicants must have a doctorate (or an equivalent degree) as well as publishing and reviewing experience. Reviewers are asked to write reviews in a timely, collegial, and constructive manner. All reviewers will begin their role on an ad-hoc basis for a period of one year, and upon successful completion of this term can be considered for full editorial review board status, with the potential for a subsequent promotion to Associate Editor.

If you have a colleague that may be interested in this opportunity, we encourage you to share this information with them.

Information Resources Management Association

Become an IRMA Member

Members of the **Information Resources Management Association (IRMA)** understand the importance of community within their field of study. The Information Resources Management Association is an ideal venue through which professionals, students, and academicians can convene and share the latest industry innovations and scholarly research that is changing the field of information science and technology. Become a member today and enjoy the benefits of membership as well as the opportunity to collaborate and network with fellow experts in the field.

IRMA Membership Benefits:

- **One FREE Journal Subscription**

- **30% Off Additional Journal Subscriptions**

- **20% Off Book Purchases**

- Updates on the latest events and research on Information Resources Management through the IRMA-L listserv.

- Updates on new open access and downloadable content added to Research IRM.

- A copy of the Information Technology Management Newsletter twice a year.

- A certificate of membership.

IRMA Membership $195

Scan code or visit **irma-international.org** and begin by selecting your free journal subscription.

Membership is good for one full year.

Printed in the United States
By Bookmasters